THE
HEALTHY
VEGETABLE
COOKBOOK

MORE THAN 175 TASTY AND
WHOLESOME RECIPES

THE
HEALTHY
VEGETABLE
COOKBOOK
MORE THAN 175 TASTY AND
WHOLESOME RECIPES

CRESCENT BOOKS
New York/Avenel, New Jersey

Fennel & Walnut Soup

Sage Derby Puffs:
3 tablespoons water
2 tablespoons butter
1/4 cup all-purpose flour
1/2 egg, beaten
3/4 cup shredded Sage Derby cheese (3 oz.)
Salt and pepper to taste
1/2 (4-oz.) pkg. cream cheese
2 tablespoons half and half

Soup:
1 tablespoon vegetable oil
1 medium-size onion, chopped
1 large bulb fennel, trimmed, chopped
3-3/4 cups vegetable stock
2 oz. walnuts, chopped
Salt and pepper to taste

To prepare puffs, preheat oven to 400F (200C). Grease a baking sheet. In a medium-size saucepan, bring water and butter to a boil. Remove from heat and beat in flour until smooth. Cool slightly, then beat in egg. Stir in 1/2 of cheese. Season with salt and pepper. In a pastry bag fitted with a small plain nozzle, pipe pea-size rounds onto greased baking sheet. Bake in preheated oven 7 to 10 minutes or until crisp. Cool slightly, then cut a slit in each round with point of a sharp knife. To prepare soup, heat oil in a large saucepan. Gently cook onion and fennel in oil until soft. Add stock and bring to a boil, then simmer 20 minutes.

Meanwhile, beat remaining cheese, cream cheese and half and half in a small bowl. Fill slits in puffs. In a food processor fitted with a metal blade or a blender, grind walnuts. Transfer ground nuts to a small dish. In food processor or blender, process soup to a smooth puree. Clean pan and return puree to pan. Stir in ground nuts and season with salt and pepper. Gently reheat. Garnish with puffs. Makes 4 to 6 servings.

Watercress & Almond Soup

2 large bunches watercress
2 tablespoons butter
1 small onion
2 cups vegetable stock
1/3 cup blanched almonds, toasted, ground
1 tablespoon plus 1 teaspoon cornstarch
2 cups milk
Salt and pepper to taste
Flaked almonds, lightly toasted, to garnish

Wash watercress. Reserve a few sprigs to garnish. Cut away any coarse stalks and chop remainder.

Melt butter in a large saucepan. Saute onion in butter until soft. Add watercress. Cook 2 minutes, then stir in chicken stock. Cover and simmer 10 minutes.

In a food processor fitted with a metal blade or a blender, process watercress mixture to a puree. Clean pan and return puree to pan. Stir in ground almonds. In a small bowl, blend cornstarch with a little milk. Add to watercress mixture, then stir in remaining milk. Simmer gently over low heat, stirring constantly, 5 minutes or until smooth. Remove from heat and cool. Refrigerate at least 4 hours or overnight. Garnish soup with flaked almonds and reserved watercress sprigs. Makes 4 servings.

Tomato & Rice Soup

1 small onion, chopped
2 garlic cloves, crushed
1 (1-lb./12-oz.) can tomatoes
2 tablespoons tomato paste
1 tablespoon chopped fresh basil or 1/2
    teaspoon dried leaf basil
2-1/2 cups water
1 teaspoon sugar
1/3 cup long-grain white rice
3 tablespoons dry sherry
Salt and pepper to taste
Fresh basil leaves to garnish

In a large saucepan, combine onion, garlic, tomatoes with juice, tomato paste, chopped basil, water and sugar. Bring to a boil, cover and simmer 30 minutes. In a food processor fitted with a metal blade or a blender, process tomato mixture to a puree. Clean pan. Pour puree through a sieve set over clean pan.

Bring back to a boil and add rice. Reduce heat and simmer 15 minutes or until rice is tender. Stir in sherry and season with salt and pepper. Garnish with basil leaves. Makes 4 to 6 servings.

Celery & Stilton Soup

1 head celery
1 medium-size onion, chopped
3 tablespoons butter
3-3/4 cups light vegetable or chicken stock
2 egg yolks
2/3 cup half and half
1 cup crumbled Blue Stilton cheese (4 oz.)
Salt and pepper to taste

Blue Cheese Croutons:
2 tablespoons butter, softened
1/3 cup shredded blue cheese (1 oz.)
1 thick slice bread

Reserve inner leaves from celery and chop remaining celery. Melt butter in a large saucepan. Gently cook celery and onion in butter, covered, until soft. Add stock and bring to a boil. Simmer 20 minutes or until vegetables are tender. Cool slightly. In a food processor fitted with a metal blade or a blender, process mixture to a puree. Clean pan and return puree to pan. Reheat gently without bringing to a boil.

Meanwhile, to prepare croutons, beat butter and shredded cheese in a small bowl. Toast bread. Spread cheese-butter on 1 side and broil until cheese-butter melts. Cut in small squares. To finish soup, beat egg yolks and half and half in a small bowl. Stir a small ladleful of hot soup into egg mixture and pour back into pan. Stir in crumbled cheese, stirring constantly until soup thickens. Season with salt and pepper. Garnish with reserved celery leaves and croutons and serve hot. Makes 4 to 6 servings.

Spicy Lentil Soup

2 tablespoons olive oil
1/2 teaspoon cumin seeds
1 medium-size onion, chopped
1 garlic clove, crushed
2 carrots, chopped
2 stalks celery, chopped
1/2 teaspoon chili powder
1/2 teaspoon turmeric
1 teaspoon ground coriander
6 oz. red lentils, washed
5 cups vegetable stock
1 bay leaf
Salt and pepper to taste
Fried onion rings and fresh tarragon sprigs to
   garnish

Heat oil in a large saucepan over medium heat. Add cumin seeds. When seeds begin to pop, add onion and cook until golden. Add garlic, carrots and celery and cook gently 10 minutes. Stir in all spices and cook 1 minute, then add lentils.

Pour in stock. Add bay leaf and bring to a boil. Reduce heat and simmer 1 hour. Remove bay leaf. In a food processor fitted with a metal blade or a blender, process soup to a puree. Clean pan and return puree to pan. Season with salt and pepper. Gently reheat. Garnish with fried onion rings and tarragon sprigs. Makes 6 servings.

Mexican Bean Soup

2 tablespoons olive oil
1 medium-size onion, chopped
1 garlic clove, crushed
1 green bell pepper, seeded, diced
12 oz. ripe tomatoes, peeled, chopped
1/2 teaspoon chili powder
3-3/4 cups vegetable stock
2 tablespoons tomato paste
1 (15-oz.) can red kidney beans, drained
Salt and pepper to taste
1 avocado
1 cup whole kernel corn
Few drops hot-pepper sauce
1 tablespoon chopped fresh cilantro
Fresh cilantro sprigs to garnish

Heat oil in a large saucepan. Cook onion until soft. Stir in garlic, bell pepper, tomatoes and chili powder. Cook 3 to 4 minutes. Pour in stock. Add tomato paste and 3/4 of beans. Simmer 30 minutes. Cool slightly. In a food processor fitted with a metal blade or a blender, process mixture to a puree.

Clean pan and return puree to clean pan. Season with salt and pepper. Cut avocado in half. Remove seed, peel and dice. Stir remaining beans, avocado, corn and hot-pepper sauce into puree. Gently reheat soup. Stir in chopped cilantro. Garnish with cilantro sprigs. Makes 4 to 5 servings.

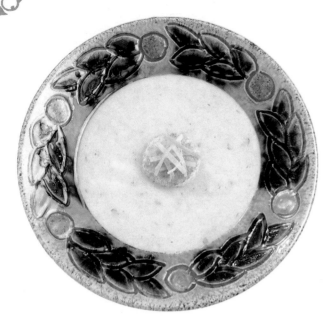

Potage Bonne Femme

1/4 cup butter
1 lb. potatoes, diced
2 carrots, chopped
2 large leeks, chopped
7-1/2 cups vegetable stock
Salt and pepper to taste
1/2 cup whipping cream
1 tablespoon finely chopped fresh parsley or
    chervil
1/2 carrot, cut in fine strips, 1/2 small leek, cut
    in fine strips and 1 slice bread, toasted, to
    garnish

Melt butter in a large saucepan. Add prepared vegetables.

Cover and cook gently 15 minutes. Add stock, bring to a boil and simmer 20 minutes. In a food processor fitted with a metal blade or a blender, process mixture to a puree. Pass through a seive set over a bowl. Clean pan and return puree to clean pan. Season with salt and pepper. Stir in whipping cream and parsley and reheat very slowly.

To prepare garnish, blanch carrot and leek strips in boiling salted water 1 minute, then drain. Cut out 4 small rounds from toast. Top toast rounds with blanched vegetables. Garnish soup with blanched vegetables and toast rounds. Makes 4 servings.

Harvest Barley Soup

1/3 cup pearl barley
5 cups vegetable stock
1 large carrot, diced
1 small turnip, diced
1 stalk celery, chopped
1 small onion, finely chopped
2 young leeks, sliced
1/2 teaspoon mixed dried herbs
1 tablespoon plus 2 teaspoons tomato paste
Salt and pepper to taste
1 bay leaf
1 (7-1/2-oz.) can butter beans, drained

Cheesey Croutons:
1 thick slice bread
1/2 cup shredded Cheddar cheese (2 oz.)

In a large saucepan, combine barley and stock. Bring to a boil and simmer 45 minutes or until barley is tender. Stir in prepared vegetables, herbs and tomato paste. Season with salt and pepper. Add bay leaf. Simmer 20 minutes. To prepare croutons, toast bread on both sides. Remove crusts and sprinkle bread with cheese. Broil until cheese is melted and golden.

Remove bay leaf and stir in beans. Gently cook 5 minutes to heat through. Cut croutons in squares and garnish soup. Makes 4 to 6 servings.

Zucchini & Tomato Soup

2 tablespoons butter
1 medium-size onion, finely chopped
12 ozs. zucchini, coarsely grated
1 garlic clove, crushed
2-1/2 cups vegetable stock
1 (14-oz.) can chopped tomatoes
2 tablespoons chopped fresh mixed herbs, if
    desired
Salt and pepper to taste
1/4 cup whipping cream and fresh basil leaves
    to garnish

Melt butter in a large saucepan. Cook onion in butter over medium heat until soft. Stir in zucchini and garlic and cook 4 to 5 minutes.

Stir in stock and tomatoes with juice. Bring to a boil and simmer 15 minutes.

Stir in herbs, if desired, and season with salt and pepper. Garnish with dollops of whipping cream and basil leaves. Makes 4 servings.

Minorcan Vegetable Soup

2 red bell peppers
2 tablespoons olive oil
1 large Spanish onion, chopped
2 garlic cloves, finely chopped
8 ozs. tomatoes, peeled, seeded, chopped
5 cups water
1 small cabbage
1/2 teaspoon dried leaf thyme
1 bay leaf
1 teaspoon paprika
Salt and pepper to taste
8 to 12 slices bread, toasted
2 garlic cloves cut in half

Broil bell peppers until skins are blisted and charred, turning over once.

Place in a plastic bag and let stand 15 minutes. Peel bell peppers, remove tops and seeds and chop. Heat oil in a large saucepan. Add onion and cook until soft. Add bell peppers, garlic and tomatoes. Cover pan and cook gently 15 minutes. Pour in water and bring to a boil.

Discard outer leaves of cabbage. Shread remaining cabbage. Add shredded cabbage, thyme, bay leaf and paprika to soup. Simmer 15 minutes. Season with salt and pepper. To serve, rub toast with a cut side of garlic. Place toast in soup bowls, then ladle hot soup over toast. Serve at once. Makes 4 to 6 servings.

Cream of Carrot Soup

2 tablespoons butter
1 small onion, finely chopped
1 medium-size potato, diced
1 lb. carrots, chopped
3 cups vegetable stock
Pinch sugar
2/3 cup half and half
Salt and pepper to taste

Herb Croutons:
2 tablespoons butter
1 teaspoon dried leaf herbs
2 slices bread

Melt butter in a large saucepan. Add onion, potato and carrots.

Cover and cook over low heat 10 minutes. Add stock and sugar. Bring to a boil, then simmer 30 minutes. In a food processor fitted with a metal blade or a blender, process mixture to a puree. Clean pan and return puree to clean pan. Stir in half and half and season with salt and pepper.

To prepare croutons, preheat oven to 400F (205C). Beat butter and herbs in a small bowl. Spread herbed butter over bread. Cut in fancy shapes or squares and place on a baking sheet. Bake in preheated oven until crisp and golden. Garnish soup with croutons. Makes 4 servings.

Tarragon & Tomato Soup

3 ozs. sorrel leaves
1 lb. ripe tomatoes
2 tablespoons olive oil
1 small onion, chopped
2 cups vegetable stock
2/3 cup dry white wine
2 egg yolks
2/3 cup half and half
Salt and pepper to taste
1 tablespoon chopped fresh tarragon
Additional half and half and fresh tarragon
    sprigs to garnish

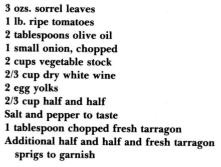

Trim stalks from sorrel and chop tomatoes. Heat oil in a large saucepan. Cook onion in oil until soft.

Add sorrel leaves and tomatoes and cook over very low heat 15 minutes. Stir in stock and wine and cook 10 minutes. Press mixture through a sieve set over a bowl. Clean pan and return puree to clean pan.

In a small bowl, beat egg yolks and half and half. Mix a small amount of puree into egg yolk mixture. Pour back into puree and reheat to thicken. Season with salt and pepper and stir in chopped tarragon. Garnish with half and half and tarragon sprigs. Makes 4 to 6 servings.

Carrot & Cilantro Soup

French Turnip Soup

1 lb. carrots
2 tablespoons olive oil
1 small onion, finely chopped
1 garlic clove, crushed
1 teaspoon coriander seeds, crushed
1 teaspoon ground coriander
3-3/4 cups vegetable stock
Salt and pepper to taste
1/3 cup dark raisins, chopped
1 tablespoons chopped fresh cilantro

Sesame Croutons:
1 thick slice bread, crusts removed
1 tablespoon butter
1 tablespoon sesame seeds

2 tablespoons butter
1 lb. small white turnips
1 small onion, chopped
5 cups vegetable stock
4 slices white bread, crusts removed
4 ozs. shelled fresh green peas
Salt and pepper to taste
Pinch grated nutmeg

Cheese Puffs:
4 ozs. puff pastry
3 tablespoons cream cheese with herbs and
   garlic
1 egg, beaten

Heat butter in a large saucepan. Add turnips and onion.

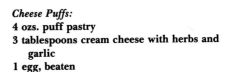

Dice 2 carrots and set aside. Chop remaining carrots. Heat oil in a large saucepan. Gently cook chopped carrots, onion and garlic in oil 10 minutes. Stir in crushed coriander seeds and ground coriander and cook 1 minute. Pour in 3 cups of stock. Cover, bring to a simmer and cook 15 minutes or until carrots are tender. Meanwhile, in a small saucepan, simmer diced carrots in remaining stock until carrots are tender.

Cook gently 10 minutes or until they begin to soften. Add stock and bread and simmer gently 25 minutes. In a food processor fitted with a metal blade or a blender, process mixture to a puree. Clean pan and return puree to clean pan. Blanch peas in boiling salted water 2 minutes, then add peas to soup. Season with salt and pepper. Add nutmeg.

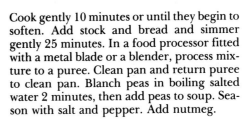

In a food processor fitted with a metal blade or a blender, process mixture to a puree. Clean pan and return puree to clean pan. Stir cooked diced carrots with stock and raisins into puree. Season with salt and pepper. Reheat gently. To prepare croutons, toast bread on each side until golden. Cool, spread with butter and sprinkle with sesame seeds. Toast until golden. Cut toast in small cubes. Stir chopped cilantro into soup. Garnish soup with sesame seed croutons. Makes 4 servings.

To prepare puffs, preheat oven to 400F (205C). Grease a baking sheet. Roll out pastry thinly and cut in 2-inch rounds. Place 1/2 teaspoon of cheese in center of each round. Dampen edge of pastry, then fold over and place on greased baking sheet. Bake in preheated oven until crisp and golden. Garnish soups with puffs. Makes 4 servings.

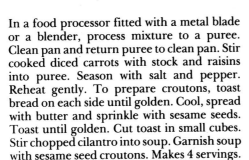

Clear Vegetable Soup

2 carrots, thinly sliced
2 stalks celery, sliced
2 ozs. button mushrooms, sliced
1-1/4 cups broccoli flowerets
1/2 cup frozen green peas
1 zucchini, cut in strips
Salt and pepper to taste
Fresh flat-leaf parsley sprigs to garnish

Vegetable Stock:
1 small onion, thinly sliced
1 leek, chopped
2 stalks celery, chopped
3 carrots, chopped
2 tomatoes, chopped
5 cups water
Bouquet garni
2 bay leaves
Salt to taste
1/2 teaspoon black peppercorns

To prepare stock, combine all stock ingredients in a large saucepan. Bring to a boil and simmer 40 minutes. For a stronger flavor, boil rapidly 5 minutes or until stock is reduced to 3-3/4 cups. Strain stock into a large bowl. Clean pan and return strained stock to clean pan. Add carrots, celery, mushrooms and broccoli. Bring to a boil. Cover and simmer 5 minutes.

Stir in green peas and zucchini and cook 2 minutes. Season with salt and pepper. Garnish with parsley sprigs. Makes 4 servings.

Winter Vegetable Soup

2 tablespoons butter
1 medium-size onion, sliced
8 ozs. carrots, diced
8 ozs. rutabagas, diced
1 medium-size potato, diced
2 large parsnips, diced
2 cups vegetable stock
1 bay leaf
1 tablespoon cornstarch
2 cups milk
Salt and pepper to taste
1 cup frozen green peas
2 small bread rolls
1/2 cup shredded Cheddar cheese (2 oz.)

Melt butter in a large saucepan. Add onion, carrots, rutabagas, potato and parsnips. Cover and cook over low heat 10 minutes. Add stock and bay leaf and simmer 30 minutes. In a small bowl, blend cornstarch with a small amount of milk, then add to soup. Pour remaining milk into soup and heat, stirring until soup thickens. Remove bay leaf and season with salt and pepper.

Stir green peas into soup and simmer over low heat. Cut bread rolls in half. Sprinkle with cheese. Broil until cheese is melted. Serve bread rolls with soup. Makes 4 servings.

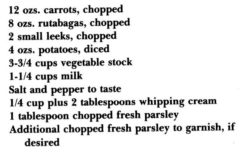

Creamy Celery & Onion Soup

Golden Vegetable Soup

1 medium-size head celery
2 medium-size onions
1/4 cup butter
1 tablespoon all-purpose flour
3 cups milk
1 bay leaf
1/4 cup crème fraiche
Salt and pepper to taste

Cut 1 stalk of celery in thin strips. Place in a bowl of iced water and set aside. Reserve several celery leaves for garnish. Reserve 1/4 of 1 onion. Chop remaining onion and remaining celery.

Melt butter in a large saucepan. Cook chopped onion and celery in butter 5 minutes. Stir in flour, then gradually blend in milk. Add bay leaf, cover and simmer 20 minutes.

12 ozs. carrots, chopped
8 ozs. rutabagas, chopped
2 small leeks, chopped
4 ozs. potatoes, diced
3-3/4 cups vegetable stock
1-1/4 cups milk
Salt and pepper to taste
1/4 cup plus 2 tablespoons whipping cream
1 tablespoon chopped fresh parsley
Additional chopped fresh parsley to garnish, if desired

In a large saucepan, combine all vegetables and stock. Bring to a boil. Cover and simmer 30 minutes.

In a food processor or a blender, process mixture to a puree. Clean pan and return puree to clean pan. Stir in milk. Reheat and season with salt and pepper.

Cool soup slightly. Remove bay leaf. In a food processor fitted with a metal blade or a blender, process soup mixture to a puree. Clean pan and return puree to clean pan. Stir in crème fraiche. Season with salt and pepper, then reheat. Chop reserved onion and stir into soup. Drain celery curls. Garnish soup with celery curls and reserved celery leaves. Makes 4 to 6 servings.

In a small bowl, whip cream until soft peaks form. Fold in 1 tablespoon chopped parsley. Top portions of soup with herb chantilly. Garnish with additional chopped parsley, if desired. Makes 4 to 6 servings.

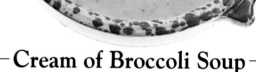

Pistou

1 tablespoon olive oil
1 medium-size onion, chopped
5 cups water
1 small potato, diced
2 carrots, sliced
2 stalks celery, finely sliced
Bouquet garni
2 small zucchini, sliced
6 ozs. green beans, cut in short lengths
1 oz. broken spaghetti or pasta shells
Salt and pepper to taste

Pistou:
3 garlic cloves
1/4 cup chopped fresh basil leaves
Salt to taste
1/2 cup freshly grated Parmesan cheese
    (1-1/2 ozs.)
2 medium-size tomatoes, peeled, seeded,
    chopped
1/4 cup olive oil

Heat 1 tablespoon oil in a large saucepan. Cook onion in oil until onion is just beginning to color. Pour in water and bring to a boil. Add potato, carrots, celery and bouquet garni. Simmer 10 minutes. Add zucchini, green beans and pasta and simmer uncovered 10 to 15 minutes or until tender.

Meanwhile, to prepare pistou, pound garlic and basil in a mortar with a pestle. Season with salt. Gradually add cheese until mixture becomes a stiff paste, then add about 1/3 of tomatoes. Continue adding cheese and tomatoes alternately, then slowly work in remaining oil to make a thick sauce. Remove bouquet garni from soup. Season with salt and pepper. Serve soup with pistou. Makes 4 to 6 servings.

Cream of Broccoli Soup

2 tablespoons butter
2 shallots, finely chopped
1 lb. broccoli flowerets, chopped
1 large potato, diced
1 garlic clove, crushed
2 cups vegetable stock
2 cups milk
Pinch grated nutmeg
Salt and pepper to taste
2/3 cup half and half, 2 tablespoons ground
    almonds and 1/4 teaspoon powdered saffron
    to garnish

Melt butter in a large saucepan. Cook shallots in butter 2 to 3 minutes or until soft. Add broccoli, potato and garlic. Cover and cook gently 5 minutes. Add stock and bring to a boil, then simmer 20 minutes or until vegetables are tender. In a food processor fitted with a metal blade or a blender, process mixture to a puree. Clean pan and return puree to clean pan. Add milk and nutmeg. Season with salt and pepper and reheat gently.

Divide half and half between 2 small bowls. Mix ground almonds into 1 bowl and saffron into other. Ladle soup into individual bowls. Garnish soup with alternate swirls of half and half mixtures. Makes 4 servings.

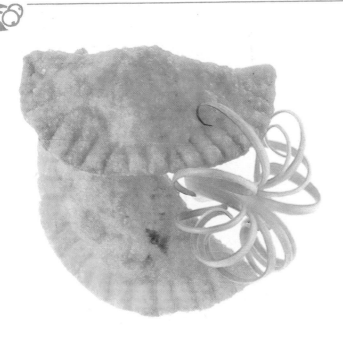

Cheese & Onion Pastries

1-1/2 cups (all-purpose) flour
1/2 teaspoon salt
1/2 cup cold water
2 tablespoons butter
1 cup chopped green onions including tops
About 1/8 teaspoon red (cayenne) pepper
4 oz. Gouda cheese
1 egg, beaten
Vegetable oil for deep-frying

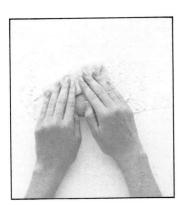

In a bowl, stir together flour and salt. Then stir in cold water to make a firm dough. Turn out onto a lightly floured surface, knead until smooth. Wrap in plastic wrap; let rest 30 minutes.

Melt butter in a skillet; add green onions. Cook, stirring, until soft. Remove from heat and stir in red pepper. Set aside. Cut cheese in 24 equal cubes. Divide dough into 24 equal portions. On a lightly floured board, roll out each portion into a 4-inch round.

Spoon green-onion mixture evenly onto dough rounds, then top each round with a cheese cube. Brush edges of each round with egg; fold in half over filling and press edges with a fork to seal. In a deep, heavy saucepan, heat about 2 inches of oil to 350F (180C) or until a 1-inch bread cube turns golden brown in about 65 seconds. Add pastries, a few at a time, and cook until golden on all sides. Drain on paper towels and serve warm. Makes 24.

Mushrooms & Blue Cheese

12 to 14 small fresh mushrooms
4 oz. blue-veined cheese
4 oz. cream cheese, room temperature
1 tablespoon half and half
Pecan halves and parsley sprigs or basil leaves

Cut stems out of mushrooms, then wipe mushrooms with a cloth dipped in cold acidulated water (1-1/2 teaspoons lemon juice or distilled white vinegar to 2 cups water). Reserve stems for other uses, if desired. Set mushrooms aside.

Crumble blue-veined cheese into a medium bowl. Add cream cheese; beat until mixture is smooth, then add half and half and beat until fluffy. Spoon into a pastry bag fitted with a star tip. If preparing ahead, refrigerate cheese mixture in pastry bag; also cover and refrigerate mushrooms.

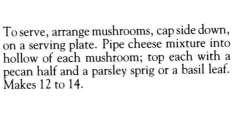

To serve, arrange mushrooms, cap side down, on a serving plate. Pipe cheese mixture into hollow of each mushroom; top each with a pecan half and a parsley sprig or a basil leaf. Makes 12 to 14.

Almond-Cheese Balls

Sesame Cheese Balls

1 cup whole blanched almonds
2 cups finely shredded Cheddar cheese (8 oz.)
1/4 cup all-purpose flour
2 egg whites
Vegetable oil for deep-frying

Coarsely chop almonds and spread on a piece of wax paper. In a bowl, lightly mix cheese and flour. In a large bowl, beat egg whites until stiff.

Sprinkle cheese-flour mixture over egg whites; gently fold together.

Form mixture into 16 to 18 equal balls. Roll cheese balls in almonds to coat; cover and refrigerate until ready to cook. To cook, in a deep, heavy saucepan, heat about 2 inches of oil to 350F (180C) or until a 1-inch bread cube turns golden brown in about 65 seconds. (Be sure oil is not too hot, or almonds will brown before centers of cheese balls are heated through.) Add cheese balls to hot oil, a few at a time, and cook until golden on all sides. Drain on paper towels and serve hot. Makes 16 to 18.

About 1/2 cup slivered almonds or pepitas
7 tablespoons sesame seeds
1 (8 oz.) pkg. cream cheese, room temperature
2 tablespoons grated Parmesan cheese
2 teaspoons instant minced onion
Salt and freshly ground pepper to taste
Tomato wedges and Italian parsley

Preheat oven to 350F (180C). Spread almonds on a baking sheet; bake about 10 minutes or until golden. Cool. Place sesame seeds in a dry skillet and stir over medium heat until golden. Remove from heat; cool.

In a bowl, beat together cream cheese, Parmesan cheese and onion. Season with salt and pepper. Cover with plastic wrap and refrigerate 20 minutes or until firm. Stir in cooled sesame seeds, then shape mixture into 25 equal balls.

Spread toasted almonds on a sheet of wax paper; roll cheese balls in nuts to coat. Arrange on a plate, cover and refrigerate (or keep in a cool place) until ready to serve. Garnish with tomato wedges and Italian parsley. Makes 25

Potted Herb Cheese

2 cups shredded Cheddar cheese (8 oz.)
2 oz. blue-veined cheese
2 tablespoons butter, room temperature
2 tablespoons dry sherry
1/2 teaspoon Worcestershire sauce
1/4 teaspoon prepared hot mustard
1 tablespoon finely chopped mixed fresh herbs
Melba toast or crackers

Place Cheddar cheese in a bowl. Crumble in blue-veined cheese; mix well with a fork. Add butter; beat to blend well.

Gradually beat in sherry, Worcestershire sauce, mustard and herbs.

Pack cheese mixture into a serving bowl, cover and refrigerate at least 1 or 2 days to allow flavor to mingle. Bring to room temperature before serving. Accompany with melba toast or crackers; provide a knife for spreading. Makes about 2-1/2 cups.

Tip: Potted cheese may be mixed in a food processor fitted with a metal blade. Process until the mixture is smooth and thoroughly mixed.

Cheese Filo Pastries

1 lb. feta cheese
3 tablespoons chopped parsley
Freshly ground pepper to taste
3 eggs, beaten
1/2 cup butter, melted
8 sheets filo pastry

Crumble cheese into a bowl. Add parsley, pepper and eggs. Mix well. Brush two 10" X 15" rimmed baking sheets with melted butter. Preheat oven to 400F (200C).

Work with 1 sheet of pastry at a time, keeping remaining pastry covered with damp paper towels or plastic wrap to prevent drying. Cut each sheet in half crosswise, then fold each half-sheet in quarters. Top folded pastry with cheese filling.

Shape pastry around filling like a money bag to enclose. Arrange pastries on buttered baking sheets and brush tops with remaining butter. Bake 20 to 25 minutes or until golden. Serve hot. Makes 16.

Deep-Fried Camembert

4 oz. Camembert cheese, well chilled
1 egg
1/2 cup fine dry bread crumbs
3/4 cup sesame seeds
Vegetable oil for deep-frying
6 fresh strawberries, if desired

Cut chilled cheese in 6 equal wedges.

In a shallow bowl, beat egg well. On a sheet of wax paper, mix bread crumbs and sesame seeds. Dip each in egg and turn to coat.

Roll cheese in crumb mixture to coat. Place on a plate. If preparing ahead, cover and refrigerate until ready to cook. To cook, in a deep, heavy saucepan, heat about 2 inches of oil to 375F (190C) or until a 1-inch bread cube turns golden brown in about 50 seconds. Add cheese wedges, a few at a time, and cook until golden on all sides. Drain on paper towels. Garnish each wedge with a strawberry, if desired. Serve warm. Makes 6 wedges.

Spinach & Feta Rolls

2 tablespoons vegetable oil
2 onions, finely chopped
1 (10-oz.) pkg. frozen chopped spinach, thawed
2 teaspoons dried dill weed
4 oz. feta cheese, crumbled
1 egg, beaten
3 tablespoons dairy sour cream
12 sheets filo pastry
1/2 cup butter, melted

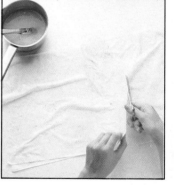

Heat oil in a saucepan over low heat. Add onions and cook, stirring occasionally, until soft but not browned. Meanwhile, drain spinach well, then place in a colander and press out as much water as possible. Stir spinach into onions and cook 2 minutes longer. Stir in dill weed and cheese.

Remove from heat; cool. Mix in egg and sour cream. Cover and refrigerate until cold. Preheat oven to 400F (200C). Work with 2 sheets of pastry at a time, keeping remaining pastry covered with damp paper towels or plastic wrap to prevent drying. Brush 1 sheet with melted butter. Top with another sheet; cut stacked sheets crosswise in 3 strips.

Place a spoonful of filling at 1 end of each strip; tuck in sides and roll up. Brush ends of rolls with melted butter; press lightly to seal. Repeat with remaining sheets of pastry to make 15 more rolls. Place rolls, seam-side down, on baking sheets. Bake about 15 minutes or until golden brown. Serve hot. Makes 18.

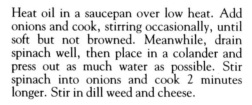

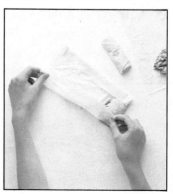

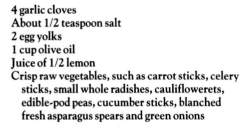

Peanut Sauce

2 garlic cloves
2 tablespoons dark soy sauce
1/4 cup smooth peanut butter
1 tablespoon sugar
1 cup water
2 small, fresh, red hot chiles, seeded
Crisp raw vegetables, such as carrots, celery,
    cucumbers, green beans, small whole radishes,
    cauliflowerets (blanched, if desired) and
    edible-pod peas

Crush garlic into a small saucepan with the soy sauce, peanut butter, sugar and water.

Cut the chiles in small slivers and add to the saucepan. Bring to a simmer; then simmer 5 minutes, stirring constantly. If sauce is very thin, simmer until slightly thickened. Remove from heat; cool to room temperature before serving. If sauce solidifies upon cooling, thin it with a little hot water.

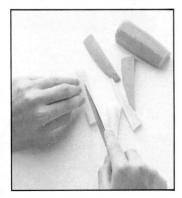

Prepare vegetables; cut carrots, celery and cucumber into 2-inch pieces, then cut in thin strips. To serve, pour sauce into a serving bowl and place in center of a platter. Arrange vegetables of your choice around sauce. Dip vegetables in sauce before eating. Makes about 1/4 cup sauce.

Aioli & Crudités

4 garlic cloves
About 1/2 teaspoon salt
2 egg yolks
1 cup olive oil
Juice of 1/2 lemon
Crisp raw vegetables, such as carrot sticks, celery
    sticks, small whole radishes, cauliflowerets,
    edible-pod peas, cucumber sticks, blanched
    fresh asparagus spears and green onions

Press garlic through a garlic press into a bowl. Add 1/2 teaspoon salt and egg yolks; beat well with a whisk. Add 1 or 2 drops oil and whisk well.

Gradually add about 2 more tablespoons oil, whisking constantly. Then, still whisking constantly, add remaining oil in a thin stream. If mixture becomes too thick, add a little hot water. When all oil has been added, whisk in lemon juice and season with additional salt, if needed. Cover aioli and refrigerate until ready to use.

Prepare the uncooked vegetables; cut the carrots in 3-inch sticks, slice the cucumber and trim the celery, radishes, cauliflowers and green onions. To serve, spoon aioli into a serving bowl and place in center of a large platter. Arrange vegetables around aioli; dip vegetables in aioli before eating. Makes about 1 cup aioli.

Marinated Artichokes

1 (14 oz.) can artichoke hearts packed in water, drained
6 tablespoons olive oil or vegetable oil
Freshly ground pepper to taste
3 tablespoons chopped mixed fresh herbs, such as parsley, basil and oregano
lemon juice and salt to taste
Toast rounds, if desired

Rinse artichoke hearts well in cold water. Drain, pat dry and cut lengthwise in halves or quarters.

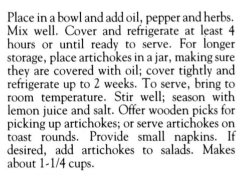

Place in a bowl and add oil, pepper and herbs. Mix well. Cover and refrigerate at least 4 hours or until ready to serve. For longer storage, place artichokes in a jar, making sure they are covered with oil; cover tightly and refrigerate up to 2 weeks. To serve, bring to room temperature. Stir well; season with lemon juice and salt. Offer wooden picks for picking up artichokes; or serve artichokes on toast rounds. Provide small napkins. If desired, add artichokes to salads. Makes about 1-1/4 cups.

Variations: For added bite, mix a few slivers of fresh, red hot chile into the marinade. If you're a garlic lover, add a crushed garlic clove.

Mexican Bean Dip

1 (15-oz) can red kidney beans
2 tablespoons vegetable oil
3/4 cup shredded Cheddar cheese (3 oz.)
Salt to taste
1 teaspoon chile powder
1 tablespoon chopped green bell pepper
Deep-fried shrimp chips, see below

Drain beans, reserving liquid.

Heat oil in a medium skillet; add drained beans and heat through, mashing with a potato masher or fork. Add 3 tablespoons reserved bean liquid and stir well. Remove from heat; cool. Stir in cheese, salt and chile powder. Heat through over low heat. If mixture is too thick, stir in more reserved bean liquid until mixture has a good consistency for scooping with chips. Stir in bell pepper. Serve dip hot, with corn or deep-fried shrimp chips. Makes about 1-1/2 cups.

Deep Fried Shrimp Chips
Shrimp chips are availabe from Asian grocery stores. Drop a few at a time into deep hot oil and when they come to the surface, remove at once; chips take only a few seconds to cook. Drain on paper towels; store in an airtight container until ready to serve.

Asparagus Rolls

25 fresh or canned asparagus spears
1 cup butter
4 egg yolks
1 tablespoon chopped fresh mint
Lemon juice to taste
25 thin slices firm-textured white bread

If using fresh asparagus, snap off and discard tough stalk ends. Wash stalks in cold water, then cook about 8 minutes in boiling water. Drain, rinse under cold running water and drain again. If using canned asparagus, drain well. Set asparagus aside.

To make sauce, melt butter in a small saucepan and keep very hot. Process egg yolks in a food processor fitted with a metal blade until frothy. With motor running, gradually add hot melted butter in a thin stream; process until blended. Transfer to a bowl; cover and refrigerate until mixture is thickened. Stir in mint and lemon juice.

Preheat broiler. Trim crusts from bread slices, then spread bread with sauce. Cut each asparagus spear in half; place 2 halves on each bread slice. Bring 2 opposite corners to center of each slice; fasten with a wooden pick. Dot with more sauce. Arrange asparagus rolls on a baking sheet; broil until crisp and golden. Makes 25.

Marinated Mushrooms

1 lb. small fresh mushrooms
1 cup water
2 teaspoons salt
1/2 cup distilled white vinegar
1 bay leaf
Few thyme sprigs
1 garlic clove
2 tablespoons olive oil
Sliced green onion or mild red onion, if desired.
Finely chopped parsley
Peel of 1 lemon, cut in thin strips

Trim mushroom stems. Wipe mushrooms with a cloth dipped in cold acidulated water (1-1/2 teaspoons lemon juice or distilled white vinegar to 2 cups water). Place mushrooms in a heatproof bowl.

In a saucepan, combine 1 cup water, salt, vinegar, bay leaf, thyme sprigs, garlic and oil. Bring to a boil; pour over mushrooms. Cool, then cover and refrigerate at least 12 hours or up to 3 days.

To serve, drain mushrooms and place in a serving bowl. Discard bay leaf, thyme and garlic. If desired, gently mix in sliced onion. Sprinkle with parsley and lemon peel. If desired, offer wooden picks for picking up mushrooms; provide small napkins. Makes about 3 cups.

Mushroom Pasties

Dolmades

1 cup plus 1 tablespoon all-purpose flour
6 tablespoons firm butter
1 to 2 tablespoons cold water
3 green onions, chopped
1/2 lb. small fresh mushrooms, chopped
1/4 teaspoon dry mustard
1 tablespoon dry sherry
2 tablespoons milk
8 pitted ripe olives, sliced
Salt and pepper to taste
1 egg, beaten

1 (8-oz.) jar grape leaves
2 tablespoons olive oil
1 onion, finely chopped
2 cups cooked long-grain white rice
Salt and pepper to taste
2 tablespoons chopped fresh mint
1 cup toasted pine nuts
Fresh mint sprigs if desired

Sift 1 cup flour into a bowl. Using a pastry blender or 2 knives, cut in 4 tablespoons butter until mixture resembles coarse crumbs. Sprinkle in cold water, stirring with a fork until dough holds together. Gather into a ball; wrap and chill 30 minutes.

Drain grape leaves and rinse well; then soak in cold water to cover to remove brine, separating leaves carefully. Drain and set aside.

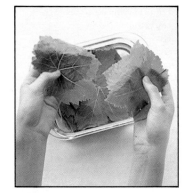

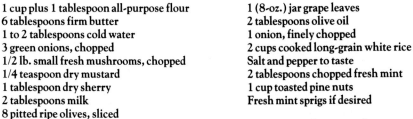

Melt remaining 2 tablespoons butter in a large skillet. Add green onions and cook, stirring, until soft but not browned. Add mushrooms and cook, stirring, until all liquid has evaporated. Stir in remaining 1 tablespoon flour; then stir in mustard, sherry and milk. Bring to a boil, stirring. Stir in olives and season. Remove from heat. Chill.

Heat oil in a medium skillet. Add onion and cook, stirring, until tender. Remove from heat and stir in rice, salt, pepper, mint and 1/2 cup toasted pine nuts. Place about 2 teaspoons filling on each leaf; roll up leaf, tucking in edges.

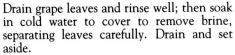

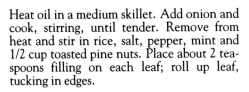

Preheat oven to 400F (200C). Grease 2 baking sheets. On a floured board, roll out pastry thinly and cut into 3-inch rounds. Place a teaspoonful of filling in center of each round. Brush up edges and join in center; pinch. Brush tops with egg. Bake 15 to 20 minutes. Makes 10.

Arrange filled leaves close together in large skillet. If necessary, make more than 1 layer; separate layers with leftover grape leaves. Pour in enough hot water to barely cover filled leaves. Place a heatproof plate directly on top of leaves; place a weight (such as canned goods) on top of plate. Cover and simmer 30 minutes. Remove from heat; cool. Cover and refrigerate until cold. Garnish with 1/2 cup toasted pine nuts or fresh mint sprigs, if desired. Makes about 45.

Feta Cheese Kebabs

7 oz. feta cheese
1/4 red bell pepper
1/4 yellow bell pepper
1 zucchini
1/4 eggplant
Thyme sprigs and pink peppercorns

Marinade:
2 tablespoons olive oil
1 tablespoon raspberry vinegar
1 teaspoon honey
1/2 teaspoon Dijon-style mustard
2 teaspoons chopped fresh thyme
1/4 teaspoon salt
1/2 teaspoon ground black pepper

To prepare marinade, combine olive oil, vinegar, peppercorns, honey, mustard, thyme, salt and pepper in a large bowl with a wooden spoon until thoroughly blended. Cut feta cheese, bell peppers, zucchini and eggplant in bite-sized pieces. Add to marinade; stir well to coat evenly. Cover with plastic wrap and refrigerate at least 1 hour.

Thread 1 piece of each ingredient onto wooden picks. Just before serving, broil under a hot grill 2 to 3 minutes or until vegetables are just tender. Garnish with thyme sprigs and peppercorns. Makes 24 kebabs.

Peppery Mozzarella Salad

6 ounces Mozzarella cheese
2 large beefsteak tomatoes, cut in half
1 ripe avocado
2 shallots, peeled, thinly sliced
1/3 cup olive oil
2 tablespoons lemon juice
1/2 teaspoon sugar
Salt to taste
1/4 to 1/2 teaspoon dry mustard
1 to 2 teaspoons green peppercorns, crushed
1/2 teaspoon dried oregano
Crusty bread or bread sticks

Thinly slice cheese and tomato and arrange on 4 small plates.

Cut avocado in thin slices and arrange with cheese and tomato. Separate shallots in rings and scatter over salad.

In a screw-topped jar, combine olive oil, lemon juice, sugar, salt, peppercorns and oregano. Shake vigorously until well blended. Spoon over salad and let marinate 1 hour. Garnish with basil, if desired, and serve with warm crusty bread or bread sticks. Makes 4 servings.

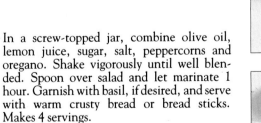

Curried Vegetable Envelopes

2 oz. puff pastry, thawed
1 egg, beaten
1 teaspoon cumin seeds
Lime twists and herb sprigs to garnish

Filling:
1 tablespoon butter
1 leek, finely chopped
1 clove garlic, crushed
1 teaspoon ground cumin
1 teaspoon garam marsala
2 teaspoons mango chutney
1/2 teaspoon finely grated lime peel
2 teaspoons lime juice
1/2 cup cooked diced potato

Preheat oven to 425F (220C). To prepare filling, melt butter in small saucepan. Add leek and garlic.

Cook quickly, stirring, 1 minute. Add cumin, garam marsala, chutney and lime peel and juice. Stir well. Cook gently 1 to 2 minutes. Add potatoes, mix well and cool. Roll out puff pastry very thinly to a 12" x 8" rectangle. Cut in 2-inch squares. Brush edge with beaten egg and place a little filling in center of each square.

Draw all corners to center and seal joins like a tiny envelope. Arrange on a baking sheet. Brush envelopes with egg to glaze and sprinkle with cumin seeds. Bake in oven 5 to 8 minutes or until well risen and golden brown. Garnish with lime twists and herb sprigs. Makes 24 pieces.

Marinated Mushrooms with Grapefruit

1 large pink grapefruit
1/3 cup ginger wine
2 teaspoons mint jelly
1/2 teaspoon salt
1/2 teaspoon ground black pepper
1 teaspoon Dijon-style mustard
48 button mushrooms
Mint leaves to garnish

Using a sharp knife, cut away grapefruit peel including white pith from flesh, allowing juice to fall into a small saucepan. Cut out segments in between membranes and place on a plate. Squeeze remaining juice from membranes into saucepan.

Stir in ginger wine, mint jelly, salt, pepper and mustard. Bring to a boil. Stir in mushrooms. Pour into a bowl and refrigerate until cold.

Cut grapefruit segments in bite-sized pieces. Reserve several grapefruit pieces for garnish. Thread mushrooms and grapefruit onto 24 wooden picks. Garnish with mint leaves and reserved grapefruit pieces. Makes 24 pieces.

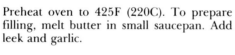

Pesto Sauce

1 cup fresh basil leaves, tightly packed
2 garlic cloves
Coarse or rock salt
2 tablespoons pine nuts
1/2 cup olive oil
2 tablespoons freshly grated Parmesan cheese
2 tablespoons freshly grated pecorino cheese, or
   2 tablespoons freshly grated Parmesan

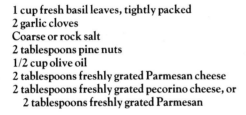

Place basil, garlic, salt and pine nuts in a blender or food processor. Whirl until finely chopped.

With motor running, add oil in a thin stream. Scrape down sides to make sure all solids are well mixed. Continue to blend until you attain a smooth sauce.

Add cheeses and give the machine one short burst to blend ingredients well. Serve hot over freshly-cooked pasta. Makes about 2 cups.

Note: Use only a high-quality olive oil and do not substitute vegetable or peanut oil. If the sauce is too thick, thin with a little of the pasta cooking water. Store any leftover sauce in a sealed container in the refrigerator for up to 1 month.

Tomato Sauce

2 lb. ripe tomatoes
1-1/2 tablespoons olive oil
1/2 cup finely chopped onions
1 celery stalk, finely chopped
2 tablespoons tomato paste
1 bay leaf
6 fresh basil leaves, or 1 teaspoon dried leaf basil
1 teaspoon sugar
1 teaspoon salt
Pepper

Dip tomatoes in boiling water to split the skin, then spear with a fork and peel. Quarter tomatoes and set aside.

In a medium heavy-based saucepan, heat oil over a low heat. Sauté onions and celery until onions are golden. Add tomatoes and any juice, tomato paste, bay leaf, basil, sugar and salt and pepper.

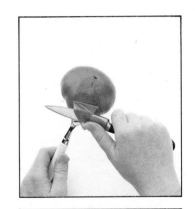

Bring to a boil. Reduce and simmer gently, uncovered, for 45 minutes, stirring occasionally. Remove bay leaf and discard. Serve hot with freshly-cooked pasta. Makes about 2-1/2 cups.

Caribbean Creole Sauce

Marinara Sauce

1/2 cup vegetable oil
2 medium onions, chopped
1 medium green bell pepper, cored, seeded, finely
    chopped
2 garlic cloves
1 teaspoon finely chopped, seeded fresh red
    chiles
1 teaspoon salt
Pepper
3 tomatoes, peeled, chopped
3/4 cup tomato paste
1/2 cup dry white wine

In a medium heavy-based saucepan, heat oil over low heat. Add onions, green pepper, garlic and chiles; sauté until the peppers are soft.

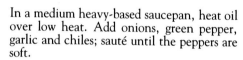

Add salt, pepper and tomatoes. Cook about 10 minutes over low heat, stirring occasionally.

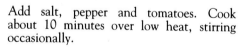

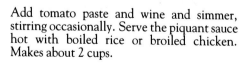

Add tomato paste and wine and simmer, stirring occasionally. Serve the piquant sauce hot with boiled rice or broiled chicken. Makes about 2 cups.

1 to 2 small fresh red chiles, such as cascabel,
    according to taste
12 large pitted, chopped, ripe olives
1 tablespoon drained capers
1/2 cup olive oil
1 medium onion, finely chopped
2 garlic cloves, finely chopped
2 teaspoons chopped fresh oregano or 1/2
    teaspoon dried leaf oregano
1 lb. ripe tomatoes or 1 lb. can peeled tomatoes

Slice each chile and use the tip of a knife to remove seeds.

In a glass or ceramic bowl, marinate the olives, chiles and capers in 4 tablespoons oil for at least 1 hour. Meanwhile, gently sauté the onion and garlic in the remaining oil until golden. Add the oregano.

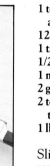

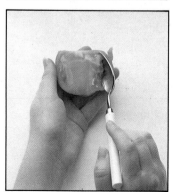

Peel fresh tomatoes; use spoon to scoop out seeds. Chop. Strain canned tomatoes. Turn all ingredients into a flameproof casserole or large skillet and cook over medium to high heat until the mixture thickens and darkens slightly. Remove chiles. Serve the sauce hot with fresh cooked pasta. Makes about 2 cups.

Tamil Nadu Vegetables

2/3 cup red split lentils
1/2 teaspoon ground turmeric
2-1/2 cups water
1 small eggplant
1/4 cup vegetable oil
1/3 cup shredded coconut
1 teaspoon cumin seeds
1/2 teaspoon mustard seeds
2 dried red chiles, crushed
1 red bell pepper, seeded, sliced
4 ounces zucchini, thickly sliced
3 ounces green beans, cut into 3/4-inch pieces
2/3 cup vegetable stock
Salt to taste
Red bell pepper strips, to garnish

Rinse lentils and put in a large pan with turmeric and water. Boil 10 minutes, then reduce heat and cover.

Simmer 15 to 20 minutes until lentils are soft. Meanwhile, cut eggplant into 1/2-inch cubes. Heat oil in a large shallow pan, add coconut, cumin seeds, mustard seeds and chiles.

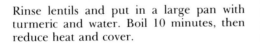
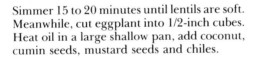

Cook 1 minute, then add eggplant, bell pepper, zucchini, green beans, stock and salt. Bring to a boil, reduce heat, cover and simmer 10 to 15 minutes, until vegetables are just tender. Stir in lentils and any cooking liquid and cook another 5 minutes. Serve hot, garnished with bell pepper strips.

Makes 4 servings.

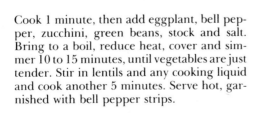

Peppers with Cauliflower

1/4 cup vegetable oil
1 large onion, sliced
2 garlic cloves, crushed
2 green chiles, seeded, chopped
1 cauliflower, cut into small flowerets
1/2 teaspoon ground turmeric
1 teaspoon garam masala
1/4 cup water
1 green bell pepper
1 red bell pepper
1 orange or yellow bell pepper
Salt and pepper to taste
1 tablespoon chopped cilantro (fresh coriander), to garnish

Heat oil in a large saucepan, add onion and cook over medium heat 8 minutes, or until soft and golden brown. Stir in garlic, chiles and cauliflowerets and cook 5 minutes, stirring occasionally. Stir in turmeric and garam masala; cook 1 minute.

Reduce heat and add water. Cover and cook 10 to 15 minutes, until cauliflower is almost tender. Meanwhile, cut peppers in half lengthwise, remove stalks and seeds and thinly slice peppers. Add to pan and cook another 3 to 5 minutes, until softened. Season with salt and pepper. Serve hot, garnished with chopped cilantro. Makes 4 servings.

Mushroom Curry

1 pound button mushrooms
2 green chiles, seeded
2 teaspoons ground coriander
1 teaspoon ground cumin
1/2 teaspoon chile powder
2 garlic cloves, crushed
1 onion, cut into wedges
2/3 cup coconut milk
Salt to taste
2 tablespoons butter
Fresh bay leaves, to garnish, if desired

Wipe mushrooms and trim stalks. Set aside.

Put chiles, coriander, cumin, chile powder, garlic, onion and coconut milk in a blender or food processor fitted with the metal blade and blend until smooth. Season to taste with salt.

Melt butter in a saucepan, add mushrooms and cook 3 to 4 minutes until golden brown. Add spice mixture, reduce heat and simmer, uncovered 10 minutes, or until mushrooms are tender. Serve hot, garnished with bay leaves, if desired. Makes 4 servings.

Dhal

1-1/4 cups brown lentils
3-3/4 cups water
1 teaspoon turmeric
1 clove garlic, crushed
2 tablespoons ghee
1 large onion, chopped
1 teaspoon garam masala
1/2 teaspoon ground ginger
1 teaspoon coriander
1/2 teaspoon cayenne pepper
Fresh cilantro sprigs, if desired

Wash lentils in cold water.

In a saucepan, combine lentils, water, turmeric and garlic. Cover and simmer 30 minutes or until lentils are tender. Uncover and cook 2 to 3 minutes to reduce excess liquid.

Heat ghee in a saucepan. Add onion and fry gently 5 minutes. Add garam masala, ginger, coriander and cayenne pepper; cook gently 1 minute. Add mixture to lentils and stir well. Garnish with cilantro, if desired. Makes 4 to 6 servings.

Note: For a less fiery flavor, reduce cayenne pepper.

Vegetable Couscous

8 ounces couscous
2 cups water
1/4 cup olive oil
2 onions, coarsely chopped
1 large eggplant, diced
1 (1 lb.) acorn squash, seeded, diced
2 carrots, sliced
1 teaspoon harissa
2 tomatoes, peeled, chopped
2 tablespoons tomato paste
2 cups vegetable stock
1 (13-oz.) can garbanzo beans, drained
2 zucchini, sliced
1/3 cup raisins
2 tablespoons chopped fresh parsley
Fresh cilantro sprig, if desired

Combine couscous and water in a bowl. Let soak 15 minutes or until water is absorbed. Heat oil in a saucepan. Add onions, eggplant, squash and carrots and fry 5 minutes, stirring frequently. Stir in harissa, tomatoes, tomato paste and stock. Bring to a boil and stir well.

Line a large metal sieve or colander with muslin or all-purpose kitchen cloth and place over pan. Spoon couscous into sieve. Cover pan with foil to enclose steam and simmer 20 minutes. Remove sieve. Add garbanzo beans, zucchini and raisins to vegetable mixture. Stir well, then replace sieve and fluff couscous with a fork. Cover again with foil and simmer 20 minutes. Spoon couscous on a large serving dish and fluff with a fork. Add parsley to vegetable mixture and spoon over couscous. Garnish with cilantro sprig, if desired, and serve hot. Makes 4 to 6 servings.

Vegetarian Lentil Medley

2/3 cup whole green lentils
2/3 cup split peas
2-1/2 cups cold water
2 leeks, cut in 1/4-inch slices
2 zucchini, cut in 1/4-inch slices
2 carrots, thinly sliced
2 stalks celery, thinly sliced
1 onion, coarsely chopped
1 clove garlic, crushed
2 tablespoons ghee
1/2 teaspoon turmeric
1 teaspoon mustard seeds
2 teaspoons garam masala
Salt to taste
Fresh celery leaves
Lemon slices

Soak lentils and peas overnight. Drain lentils and peas and put into a saucepan. Add cold water, bring to a boil and boil 10 minutes. Add vegetables and garlic, cover and cook gently 10 minutes.

Meanwhile, melt ghee in a saucepan. Add turmeric, mustard seeds and garam masala and cook gently 2 minutes or until seeds begin to pop. Stir into lentil mixture and cook 15 minutes or until vegetables and lentils are tender and liquid has been absorbed. Season with salt. Garnish with celery leaves and lemon slices and serve hot. Makes 4 servings.

1 cup (4 oz.) all-purpose flour
Pinch of salt
2 eggs
1-1/4 cups milk
1 tablespoon butter, melted

Vegetable oil
Lemon juice and sugar *or* **warmed jam**

Sift flour and salt into a bowl. Make a well in the center and add the eggs and a little of the milk. Beat well with a wooden spoon, working in all the flour. Gradually beat in the remaining milk until bubbles form on top of batter. Stir in butter.

Add a small amount of oil to a 7-inch crepe pan—enough to barely cover the base—and place over high heat. Pour in 2 to 3 tablespoons batter and quickly tilt the pan so that the batter covers the base thinly and evenly. Cook for about 1 minute over high heat until lightly browned underneath.

Whole-Wheat Crepes

1 cup (4 oz.) whole-wheat flour
1/2 teaspoon salt
3 eggs
1-1/4 cups milk

Vegetable oil
Assorted savory or sweet toppings

Stir flour and salt in a bowl. Make a well in the center and add the eggs and a little of the milk. Beat well with a wooden spoon, working in all the flour. Gradually beat in the remaining milk until bubbles form on top of the batter.

Add a small amount of oil to a 7-inch crepe pan – enough to barely cover the base – and place over high heat. Pour in 2 to 3 tablespoons batter and quickly tilt the pan so that the batter covers the base thinly and evenly. Cook for about 1 minute over high heat until lightly browned underneath. Turn crepe with a metal spatula and cook other side for about 30 seconds. Keep crepe warm. Continue until batter is used. Serve with savory or sweet toppings. Makes 8 crepes.

Turn crepe with a metal spatula and cook other side for about 30 seconds. Keep crepe warm. Continue until batter is used. Serve with lemon juice and sugar, or with warmed jam. Makes 8 crepes.

Mozzarella & Crouton Crepes

7-inch crepes (page 32)

1/4 cup butter
1 (1-inch) thick slice bread, cubed
1 cup (4 oz.) diced Mozzarella cheese
Salt and pepper
1/3 cup grated parmesan cheese
Basil sprigs

Keep crepes warm while preparing filling. Heat butter in a small skillet over medium heat. Add bread cubes and cook, stirring often, until golden. Remove from heat and stir in Mozzarella. Season with salt and pepper.

Preheat broiler. Divide filling between crepes. Roll up and arrange in a single layer in a shallow heatproof dish. Sprinkle with Parmesan. Broil until lightly browned, about 2 minutes. Garnish with sprigs of basil. Serves 4.

Parmesan Crepes

7-inch crepes (page 32)

2 tablespoons vegetable oil
2 tablespoons butter
1/2 lb. potatoes, cooked and diced
Salt and pepper
1 cup fresh bread crumbs
1/4 cup butter, melted
1 tablespoon chopped fresh parsley
2/3 cup grated Parmesan cheese
Parsley sprigs

Keep crepes warm while preparing filling. Heat oil and 2 tablespoons butter in a medium-size skillet over medium-high heat. Add potatoes and cook until crisp and golden; drain well. Season with salt and pepper.

Preheat broiler. Spoon potatoes in center of crepes. Roll up and arrange in a single layer in a shallow heatproof dish. In a small bowl, combine bread crumbs, melted butter and chopped parsley; sprinkle over crepes. Top with Parmesan. Broil about 6 inches from heat source until crisp and golden, 4 to 5 minutes. Garnish with sprigs of parsley. Serves 4.

Asparagus Crepes

7-inch crepes (page 32)
12 fresh or canned asparagus tips, plus
   additional asparagus tips for garnish, if
   desired
2 tablespoons butter
2 teaspoons all-purpose flour
2/3 cup half and half
1 teaspoon chopped fresh parsley
1 teaspoon chopped fresh chives
Salt and pepper
1 tablespoon grated Parmesan cheese

Keep crepes warm while preparing filling. If asparagus is fresh, cook in boiling salted water until crisp-tender, about 6 minutes; drain well. If aspara-gus is canned, drain well. Melt butter in a small saucepan over low heat. Stir in flour and cook 30 seconds. Stir in half and half and cook, stirring frequently, until thick. Stir in parsley, chives, salt and pepper.

Preheat broiler. Set aside any asparagus being used for garnish; stir remaining asparagus into sauce. Divide filling between crepes. Roll up and arrange in a single layer in a shallow heatproof dish. Top with reserved asparagus and sprinkle with Parmesan. Broil until cheese is melted and lightly browned, about 2 minutes. Serves 4.

Crepes with Corn-Cheese Sauce

7-inch crepes (page 32)

1 medium-size onion, finely chopped
2 tablespoons butter
1 (14-oz.) can corn, drained
3 cups basic cheese sauce
1 teaspoon chopped fresh marjoram
1/4 cup (1 oz.) shredded Cheddar cheese
Marjoram sprigs

Keep crepes warm while preparing filling. In a medium-size saucepan, combine onion and butter. Cook over low heat until onion is softened, about 5 minutes. Stir in corn and heat through. Reserve 6 tablespoons cheese sauce; add remaining sauce and the chopped marjoram to pan.

Preheat broiler. Place one crepe on a large heatproof plate. Spread with some of the corn mixture. Top with a second crepe. Repeat until all crepes are used, finishing with a crepe on top. Top with reserved cheese sauce and sprinkle with Cheddar. Broil until sauce is bubbling, about 3 minutes. To serve, cut in wedges. Garnish with marjoram sprigs. Serves 4.

Mushroom Crepes

7-inch crepes (page 32)

1/4 cup butter
1/2 lb. mushrooms, thinly sliced
1/2 cup all-purpose flour
1-1/4 cups milk
1/4 teaspoon grated nutmeg
Salt and pepper
Chopped parsley and parsley sprigs

Keep crepes warm while preparing filling. Melt butter in a medium-size saucepan over low heat. Add all but 4 mushroom slices; cover and cook 5 minutes. Stir in flour and cook 1 minute. Gradually stir in milk. Bring to a boil, stirring constantly, then simmer 3 minutes. Season with nutmeg, salt and pepper.

Preheat oven to 350F (175C). Divide filling between crepes. Roll up and arrange in a single layer in a shallow heatproof dish. Cover with foil. Bake 20 minutes. Garnish with reserved mushroom slices and parsley. Serves 4.

Spinach Crepes

7-inch crepes (page 32)

2 lbs. fresh spinach, well-washed

2 tablespoons butter
1 medium-size onion, finely chopped
1 tablespoon tomato puree
1 teaspoon paprika
2 hard-cooked eggs, chopped
Salt and pepper
1/3 cup grated Parmesan cheese
Parsley sprigs

Keep crepes warm while preparing filling. Wash spinach thoroughly. Place in a large pan, using only water that clings to leaves. Cover and cook over low heat until spinach is tender and limp. Drain well, then press out as much moisture as possible. Chop spinach finely; set aside.

Melt butter in a medium-size saucepan over low heat. Add onion and cook until soft, about 5 minutes. Stir in tomato puree and paprika and simmer 2 minutes. Stir in eggs. Season with salt and pepper. Preheat broiler. Divide spinach between crepes and spread evenly. Top with egg mixture. Roll up and arrange in a single layer in a shallow heatproof dish. Sprinkle with Parmesan. Broil until lightly browned, about 2 minutes. Garnish with parsley sprigs. Serves 4.

3 eggs
Salt and pepper
1 tablespoon butter

In a small bowl, beat eggs with salt and pepper until just mixed. Set 7-inch omelet pan over low heat to become thoroughly hot.

Add butter to pan. When butter is sizzling but not brown, pour in eggs. Using a fork or spatula, draw mixture from sides to middle of pan, allowing uncooked egg to run underneath. Repeat two or three times so egg rises slightly and becomes fluffy. Cook until golden-brown underneath and top is still slightly runny, about 2 minutes.

Using a metal spatula, fold over 1/3 of mixture away from handle. Holding the handle with the palm of the hand on top, place the pan over a warm serving plate. Shake omelet to edge of pan and tip completely over to make another fold. Garnish with a sprig of watercress and a tomato wedge, if desired. Serve immediately. Serves 1.

Curried Omelet

2 tablespoons butter
1 medium-size onion, finely chopped
2 teaspoons curry powder
1 eating apple, peeled, cored and diced
1 tablespoon mango chutney, finely
    chopped
Salt and pepper
Squeeze of lemon juice

Basic Omelet (see left)

Prepare filling before making omelet. Melt butter in a medium-size skillet over low heat. Add onion and cook 3 minutes. Stir in curry powder and apple and continue cooking, stirring occasionally, 5 minutes. Stir in chutney. Season with salt, pepper and lemon juice. Keep warm.

Make omelet. Spoon filling over half the omelet. Fold over, cut in half and serve immediately. Garnish with apple slices and coriander sprigs, if desired. Serves 2.

Italian Omelet

Filling:
4 tablespoons butter
1 small onion, finely chopped
1 medium-size tomato, peeled and
  chopped
1 tablespoon chopped green pepper

Omelet:
3 eggs
2 oz. (1/3 cup) cooked pasta
Salt and pepper
2 tablespoons grated Parmesan cheese
Basil leaves

Prepare filling before making omelet. Melt 2 tablespoons butter in a small saucepan over low heat. Add onion and cook, stirring occasionally, 2 minutes. Stir in tomato and green pepper. Cover and cook 10 minutes.

Preheat broiler. In a small bowl, beat eggs until just mixed. Stir in pasta. Season with salt and pepper. Set 7-inch omelet pan over low heat to become thoroughly hot. Add remaining butter to pan. When butter is sizzling but not brown, pour in egg mixture. Using a fork or spatula, draw mixture from sides to middle of pan, allowing uncooked egg to run underneath. Repeat two or three times until egg rises slightly and becomes fluffy. Cook until golden-brown underneath and top is slightly runny, about 2 minutes.

Spread filling over half the omelet. Fold over and sprinkle with Parmesan. Broil just long enough to melt cheese, about 30 seconds. To serve, cut in half and garnish with basil. Serves 2.

Florentine Omelet

4 oz. fresh spinach, well-washed
1-1/2 cups basic cheese sauce

Basic Omelet (page 36)

1/2 cup (2 oz.) shredded Cheddar cheese
Cayenne pepper

Prepare filling before making omelet. Cook spinach in a small saucepan over low heat until very tender. Drain well; press out excess moisture. Warm cheese sauce.

Preheat broiler. Make omelet. Spoon spinach over half the omelet. Fold over and lift onto a warm heatproof plate. Spoon cheese sauce over top; sprinkle with cheese and cayenne. Broil until sauce is bubbling and lightly browned. Serves 1.

Broccoli Pasta Soufflé

8 oz. broccoli
3 tablespoons butter
3 tablespoons all-purpose flour
1-1/4 cups milk
3/4 cup shredded Cheddar
  cheese (3 oz.)
Salt, pepper and nutmeg
4 egg whites
3 egg yolks
2 cups pasta shells (4 oz.), cooked

Divide broccoli in small flowerets. Cook in a medium-size saucepan in a small amount of boiling salted water until crisp-tender. Drain. Preheat oven to 400F (205C). In a large saucepan, melt butter; stir in flour. Cook 2 minutes, stirring constantly, over low heat. Gradually stir in milk. Cook,
stirring constantly, until sauce thickens. Simmer gently 5 minutes. Stir in cheese. Season with salt, pepper and nutmeg. Let cool slightly. In a large bowl, whisk egg whites until stiff but not dry. Stir egg yolks into cheese sauce, then stir in broccoli and pasta. Stir 1 tablespoon of egg whites into mixture; gently fold in remaining egg whites. Grease a 2-quart soufflé dish (7-3/4" x 3-3/4"). Pour in mixture; bake about 30 minutes or until soufflé is well risen, golden brown and just set in middle. Serve at once. Makes 4 servings.

Note: This mixture may be baked in individual soufflé dishes 20 minutes.

Vegetarian Bolognese Sauce

2-3/4 cups water
1 cup lentils (6 oz.)
2/3 cup split peas (4 oz.)
2 tablespoons vegetable oil
1 onion, finely chopped
1 garlic clove, crushed
1 carrot, finely chopped
1 celery stalk, finely chopped
1 (15-oz.) can tomatoes, drained,
  chopped
1 teaspoon dried leaf oregano
Salt and pepper

In a medium-size saucepan, bring water to a boil. Stir in lentils and split peas. Simmer, covered, about 40
minutes or until all liquid has been absorbed and lentils and peas are soft. In a medium-size saucepan, heat oil. Add onion, garlic, carrot and celery. Cook over low heat, stirring occasionally, until soft. Stir in tomatoes and oregano. Season with salt and pepper. Cover pan; simmer gently 5 minutes. Add cooked lentils and split peas to vegetable mixture. Cook, stirring occasionally, until well combined and heated through. Makes 4 to 6 servings.

Note: Serve with whole-wheat spaghetti, if desired.

Marinated Stuffed Leaves

8 small spinach leaves
8 small Chinese cabbage leaves
8 small radichio leaves
1 (8-oz.) pkg. cream cheese, softened
1 garlic clove, crushed
2 tablespoons chopped fresh parsley
1 yellow bell pepper
Fresh herb sprigs and shredded orange
    peel to garnish

Marinade:
1 teaspoon finely grated orange peel
1 tablespoon fresh orange juice
1/3 cup olive oil
1 tablespoon chopped fresh marjoram
1/2 teaspoon salt
1/2 teaspoon black pepper
1 teaspoon Dijon-style mustard
1 teaspoon superfine sugar

Plunge spinach leaves into boiling water 30 seconds. Using a slotted spoon, remove leaves and refresh in cold water. Drain well. Repeat with Chinese and radichio leaves, keeping each separate. To prepare marinade, in a large bowl, combine all marinade in-gredients until well blended. Pour 1/3 of marinade into a separate medium-size bowl. Add radichio leaves to sepa-rate bowl, turning leaves in to marinade to coat. Place spinach and Chinese leaves in remaining marinade, turning leaves to coat evenly. Cover and re-frigerate 2 hours. To prepare filling, in a small bowl, beat cream cheese, garlic and parsley until evenly blended. Cover and refrigerate until needed. Preheat oven to 425F (220C). Bake bell pepper on a baking sheet in preheated oven 15 to 20 minutes or until skin is charred. Peel bell pepper and remove stalk and seeds. In a food processor fit-ted with a metal blade, process bell pep-per until smooth. Drain leaves, reserv-ing marinade. Spread out 1 leaf at a time flat on a cutting board. Place 1 teaspoonful of cream cheese mixture in center, fold in edges and roll up firmly. Repeat with remaining leaves and cream cheese mixture. Place on a serv-ing dish. Combine bell pepper and remaining marinade. Pour around leaves in dish. Garnish with herb sprigs and orange peel. Makes 4 servings.

Mixed Vegetable Kebabs

1 (12-oz.) eggplant, cut in bite-size pieces
Salt
1 small red bell pepper, seeded, cut in
    3/4-inch squares
1 small yellow bell pepper, seeded, cut
    in 3/4-inch squares
4 small zucchini, trimmed, cut in
    1/2-inch slices
8 shallots, each cut in 4 pieces
16 button mushrooms
16 cherry tomatoes
Fresh oregano sprigs to garnish

Marinade:
1/3 cup olive oil
1 tablespoon raspberry vinegar
1/2 teaspoon black pepper
1/2 teaspoon salt
1 teaspoon dry mustard powder
1 tablespoon light-brown sugar
1 tablespoon chopped fresh oregano
1 tablespoon chopped fresh parsley

Soak 8 wooden skewers in cold water. To prepare marinade, in a large bowl, combine all marinade ingredients until well blended. Place eggplant in a col-ander or sieve set over a bowl. Sprinkle with salt. Cover with a plate to weight and let stand 30 minutes. Rinse egg-plant thoroughly to remove salt, then press out excess water. Add all vegeta-bles to marinade, turning vegetables carefully to coat completely. Cover and refrigerate 1 hour. Meanwhile, prepare a barbecue. Thread a mixture of vege-tables onto presoaked skewers. Cook 3 to 5 minutes or until vegetables are just tender, brushing with marinade. Gar-nish with oregano. Makes 8 servings.

Ratatouille

1 small eggplant, thinly sliced
Salt
1/3 cup olive oil
1 small red bell pepper, seeded,
   thinly sliced
1 small yellow bell pepper, seeded,
   thinly sliced
2 medium-size onions, thinly sliced
3 small zucchini, thinly sliced
3 medium-size tomatoes, peeled, seeded,
   thinly sliced
Fresh herb sprigs to garnish

Marinade:
2 tablespoons red wine
1 garlic clove
2 tablespoons chopped fresh cilantro
2 tablespoons chopped fresh basil
2 tablespoons chopped fresh parsley
1 teaspoon Dijon-style mustard
1/2 teaspoon salt
1/2 teaspoon black pepper

Arrange eggplant in a sieve set over a bowl, sprinkling between layers with salt. Cover with a plate to weight and let stand 30 minutes. Rinse under cold running water. Dry on paper towels. Heat olive oil in a large skillet. Saute eggplant, peppers, onions and zucchini, stirring occasionally, 4 to 5 minutes or until vegetables are almost tender. Add tomatoes. Cook 3 to 4 minutes or until vegetables are tender. To prepare marinade, in a large bowl, combine all marinade ingredients until well blended. Add vegetables, turning vegetables in marinade to completely coat. Let stand until cold. Garnish with herb sprigs. Makes 6 servings.

Spiced Okra

3/4 lb. okra, washed, ends removed
4 medium-size tomatoes, peeled, seeded,
   chopped
2/3 cup water
1/2 cup plain yogurt
Fresh flat-leaf parsley sprigs to garnish

Marinade:
1 red chili pepper, seeded, chopped
1 onion, finely chopped
1 garlic clove, crushed
1 teaspoon ground cumin
1 teaspoon ground coriander
1/2 teaspoon salt
1/2 teaspoon black pepper
1 teaspoon sugar
2 tablespoons olive oil

To prepare marinade, in a large bowl, combine all marinade ingredients until well blended. Add okra to marinade, turning okra carefully until evenly coated. Cover and refrigerate 1 hour. In a large saucepan, bring tomatoes and water to a boil. Add okra and marinade. Bring to a boil, stirring carefully, then cover and simmer 15 to 20 minutes or until okra is tender. Remove okra with a slotted spoon and arrange on a serving plate. Drain tomato mixture. Gently combine yogurt and tomato mixture. Spoon tomato mixture onto spiced okra. Garnish with parsley sprigs and serve hot or cold. Makes 4 to 6 servings.

Traditional Pizza Dough

2-3/4 cups bread flour
1 teaspoon salt
1 teaspoon active dried yeast
1 teaspoon sugar
About 3/4 cup warm water (110F, 45C)
1 tablespoon olive oil

Sift flour and salt into a medium bowl.

In a small bowl, combine yeast, sugar and 1/4 cup water; leave until frothy. Add yeast liquid to flour with remaining water and oil. Mix to a soft dough; knead on a floured surface 10 minutes until smooth. Place in a greased bowl; cover with plastic wrap. Let rise in a warm place 45 minutes or until doubled in size.

Punch down dough and knead briefly. Oil a 12-inch pizza pan. Place dough in center of pan; press out to edges with your knucles. Pinch up edges to make a rim. Use as directed in recipe.

Three Pepper Pizza

1 recipe Traditional Pizza Dough, shaped and ready for topping, see left

Topping:
1 red pepper
1 yellow bell pepper
1 green bell pepper
2 tomatoes, peeled
3 tablespoons olive oil
1 onion, finely chopped
1 garlic clove, crushed
Salt and pepper
Pinch of dried leaf oregano
Oregano sprigs and olives, to garnish

Make the topping. Peel peppers; spear one at a time with a fork and hold over a gas flame for 5 to 10 minutes until black and blistered. Or, halve and seed peppers. Place under preheated grill until back. Peel skin off with a knife.

Chop red pepper; quarter, seed and chop tomatoes. Put in a saucepan with 2 tablespoons oil, onion and garlic. Cook until soft. Preheat oven to 425F (220C). Brush dough with a little oil.

Spread red pepper mixture over dough. Season to taste with salt and pepper. Sprinkle with oregano. Cut remaining peppers in strips. Arrange over pizza. Season to taste with salt and pepper. Drizzle with remaining oil. Bake 20 minutes until dough is crisp and golden. Garnish with oregano sprigs and olives. Makes 4 servings.

Four Cheese Pizza

1 recipe Traditional Pizza Dough, shaped and ready for topping, page 45

Topping:
2 tablespoons olive oil
2 ounces mozzarella cheese
2 ounces Gorgonzola cheese
2 ounces Fontina or Gruyère cheese
1/2 cup freshly grated Parmesan cheese
Salt and pepper
Chopped green onion and grated Parmesan cheese, to garnish

Preheat oven to 425F (220C). Brush dough with 1 tablespoon oil. Cut the first 3 cheeses into small cubes. Scatter over the dough. Sprinkle with Parmesan cheese; season to taste with salt and pepper. Drizzle with remaining oil.

Bake 20 minutes until cheese is melted and dough is crisp and golden. Garnish with green onion and additional Parmesan chese. Makes 4 servings.

Eggplant & Tomato Pizza

1 recipe Traditional Pizza Dough, shaped and ready for topping, page 45

Eggplant Topping:
1 pound eggplants
1 garlic clove, crushed
3 tablespoons lemon juice
3 tablespoons chopped fresh parsley
2 green onions, chopped
Salt and pepper

To Finish:
1 pound tomatoes, sliced
1 tablespoon olive oil
2 tablespoons chopped fresh parsley
2 tablespoons freshly grated Parmesan cheese
Parsley sprigs, to garnish

First make Eggplant Topping. Preheat oven to 350F (175C). Put eggplants on a baking sheet and bake 30 minutes, until soft. Cool. Halve and scoop out soft centers into a bowl. Add garlic, lemon juice, parsley and green onions. Season to taste with salt and pepper.

Increase oven temperature to 425F (220C). Spread Eggplant Topping over dough. Arrange sliced tomatoes on top, brush with oil and season to taste with salt and pepper. Sprinkle with chopped parsley and Parmesan cheese. Bake 20 minutes until crust is golden. Garnish with parsley sprigs. Makes 4 servings.

Note: Eggplant Topping may be made in advance and refrigerated for 3 to 4 days. It is also delicious served as a dip with hot toast or pita bread.

Artichoke & Cheese Pizza

1 recipe Traditional Pizza Dough, shaped
   and ready for topping, page 45

Topping:
3 tablespoons olive oil
1 (14-oz.) can artichoke hearts
Salt and pepper
2 cups (8 oz.) shredded Emmental cheese
Marjoram leaves and sliced pimento, to
   garnish

Preheat oven to 425F (220C). Brush
the pizza dough with 1 tablespoon of
the oil.

Drain artichokes and slice thinly.
Arrange artichoke slices over dough.
Sprinkle with remaining oil; season to
taste with salt and pepper. Sprinkle the
cheese over the top.

Bake 20 minutes until crust is crisp and
golden and cheese has melted. Garnish
with marjoram leaves and sliced
pimento. Serve at once. Makes 4
servings.

Leek & Onion Calzone

1 recipe Traditional Pizza Dough, made to
   end of step 2, page 45

Filling:
3 tablespoons olive oil
2 small leeks, sliced
2 onions, sliced
1 large Spanish onion, sliced
1/2 cup dry white wine
1/2 cup half and half
Salt and pepper
Freshly grated nutmeg
4 ounces stuffed olives, chopped
1 tablespoon olive oil
Leek, onion and olive halves, to garnish

In a medium saucepan, heat 3 tablespoons oil over low heat. Add leeks and
onions; cook 10 minutes until soft.
Increase heat, add wine and cook until
almost dry.

Reduce heat; add half and half. Season
to taste with salt, pepper and nutmeg.
Cook 2 to 3 minutes until creamy.
Remove from heat, stir in chopped
olives and set aside.

Preheat oven to 425F (220C). Grease
2 baking sheets. Divide dough into 2
equal pieces. Roll out each piece on a
lightly floured surface to a 10-inch
circle. Brush lightly with 1 tablespoon
oil.

Divide filling between the 2 dough
pieces, confining it to one half of each
circle. Dampen edges with water, then
fold dough over to enclose filling and
seal well by pressing with a fork.
Transfer to baking sheets, brush with
beaten egg and make 2 or 3 air holes
with a sharp knife. Bake 20 minutes
until golden. Garnish with leek, onion
and olive slices. Makes 4 to 6 servings.

Stilton & Walnut Salad

2 medium heads Belgian endive
2 heads Little Gem lettuce, shredded, or
  about 4 cups shredded inner romaine
  lettuce leaves
1 large ripe pear
2 oz. Blue Stilton cheese, grated (about
  1/2 cup)
Walnut Dressing, see below
Walnut halves

Walnut Dressing:
1/2 cup walnut pieces
1/4 cup sunflower oil
2 tablespoons lemon juice
2 tablespoons apple juice
Salt and black pepper to taste

Chop endive and place in a bowl with shredded lettuce. Peel, quarter and core pear; then cut each quarter into thin slices. Add pear and cheese to endive and lettuce; toss to mix. To prepare Walnut Dressing, place all dressing ingredients in a blender and process until smooth. Pour dressing over salad and toss together. Divide salad among 4 plates and garnish with walnut halves. Makes 4 servings.

Malaysian Salad

Peanut Sauce, see below
About 3 cups shredded green cabbage
4 oz. thin green beans, ends trimmed, cut
  into 1-inch lengths
1/2 small cauliflower, broken into small
  flowerets
About 2 cups fresh bean sprouts
1/2 cucumber
Fresh cilantro (coriander) leaves

Peanut Sauce:
1/3 cup unsweetened grated coconut
2/3 cup boiling water
3 tablespoons peanut butter
2 teaspoons soy sauce
Juice of 1/2 lime
1/4 teaspoon chili powder

To prepare Peanut Sauce, place coconut in a bowl and pour boiling water over it. Let soak 15 minutes. Pour mixture through cheesecloth into another bowl, pressing to extract liquid (discard coconut). Add remaining sauce ingredients; mix well. Set aside. Fill a large saucepan with water; bring to a boil. Add cabbage, beans and cauliflower; boil 2 to 3 minutes. Drain vegetables thoroughly; arrange on a platter or 4 individual plates. Scatter bean sprouts over vegetables. Score sides of cucumber deeply with a fork or cut strips of peel from sides with a vegetable peeler. Slice cucumber; arrange around salad. Spoon Peanut Dressing onto center of salad or serve separately. Garnish salad with cilantro. Makes 4 servings.

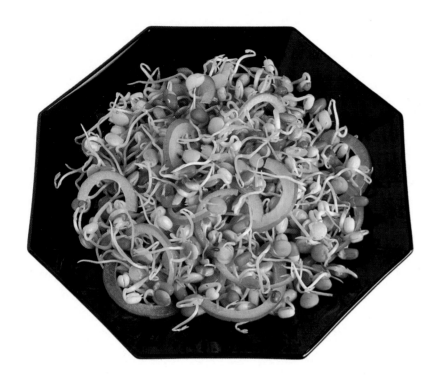

Sprouted Bean Salad

About 1/4 cup adzuki beans
About 1/4 cup mung beans
About 1/4 cup green lentils
1 red onion
Honey & Mustard Dressing, see below

Honey & Mustard Dressing:
1/4 cup mayonnaise
2 tablespoons sunflower oil
1 teaspoon honey
1 tablespoon mild prepared mustard
1 tablespoon lemon juice
Salt and black pepper to taste.

Put adzuki beans, mung beans and lentils in 3 separate bowls. Cover with water and let soak overnight; then drain each and put in a wide-mouth jar. Cover jars with cheesecloth; secure cloth with rubber bands. Set jars in a warm, dark place 4 to 6 days or until beans and lentils have sprouted; twice a day, fill jars with water and drain through cloth to rinse beans and lentils. Remove sprouts from jars, rinse again, drain and store in refrigerator up to 4 days. To serve, cut onion in half lengthwise, then thinly slice crosswise. Mix onion and sprouts in a serving dish. Prepare Honey & Mustard Dressing by beating together all dressing ingredients until honey is evenly blended. Pour dressing over salad, toss and serve. Makes 6 side-dish servings.

Jade Salad

1 cup plus 2 tablespoons long-grain white rice
8 oz. frozen chopped spinach (about 3/4 of a 10-oz. pkg.), thawed
2 tablespoons chopped parsley
6 to 8 green onions, trimmed
Vinaigrette dressing, to taste
Salt and black pepper to taste
Green onion brush

Following package directions, cook rice in boiling salted water until tender. Drain, rinse with cold water and drain again. While rice is cooking, squeeze as much water out of spinach as possible; then place spinach in a bowl and add parsley. Reserve 2 green onions; finely chop remaining onions and add to spinach. Add warm cooked rice to spinach mixture; stir in vinaigrette dressing. Season with salt and pepper. Let salad cool completely, then refrigerate before serving. Makes 6 first-course or side-dish servings.

Tabbouleh

1 cup bulgur (cracked wheat)
1/4 cup lemon juice
1/4 cup virgin olive oil
Salt and black pepper to taste
1 tablespoon finely chopped mild white
    or yellow onion
6 green onions, finely chopped
1 small bunch flat-leaf parsley, trimmed,
    chopped
About 3/4 cup chopped fresh mint
1 head romaine lettuce
Cherry tomatoes
Flat-leaf parsley sprigs

Place bulgur in a bowl and add warm water to cover. Let soak 30 minutes. Squeeze out excess water; put bulgur in a bowl. Add lemon juice, oil, salt and pepper, white or yellow onion, green onions, chopped parsley and mint. Mix to combine well, then refrigerate at least 1 hour before serving. To serve, arrange lettuce leaves around edge of a platter; spoon tabbouleh in center of platter and garnish with tomatoes and parsley sprigs. Makes 6 side-dish servings.

Waldorf Salad

3 red-skinned apples
2 tablespoons lemon juice
5 celery stalks, thinly sliced
About 1/2 cup coarsely chopped walnuts
1/2 teaspoon caraway seeds
1/2 cup mayonnaise
Walnut halves
Celery leaves

Core and dice apples, then place in a bowl and toss with lemon juice to prevent discoloration. Add sliced celery, chopped walnuts and caraway seeds. Toss to mix, then stir in mayonnaise. Spoon salad into a salad bowl, garnish with walnut halves and celery leaves and serve. Makes 6 side-dish servings.

Beet & Onion Salad

1 lb. beets, cooked, peeled, cut into thin
   julienne strips
2 shallots, finely chopped
1/4 cup vinaigrette dressing
Lettuce leaves of your choice
1/2 small onion, thinly sliced, separated
   into rings
1 tablespoon chopped parsley

In a glass dish, mix beets, shallots and
vinaigrette dressing. Let marinate 2
hours. Line a serving dish with lettuce
leaves; spoon in salad and scatter
onions on top. Garnish with parsley
and serve. Makes 4 to 6 servings.

Whole Wheat Pasta Salad

4 oz. dried whole wheat pasta twists or
   other shapes
6 oz. shelled fresh lima or fava beans (or
   use about 1-1/4 cups frozen baby green
   lima beans)
About 2 cups fresh broccoli flowerets
3 oz. snow peas, ends and strings removed
3 tomatoes, diced
Vinaigrette dressing flavored with garlic,
   to taste
1 teaspoon chopped fresh oregano

Following package directions, cook
pasta in boiling salted water until
tender but still firm. Drain, rinse with
cold water and drain again. Set aside to
cool. Cook fresh lima or fava beans in
boiling water 20 to 25 minutes or until
tender; drain. While beans are still
warm, slip off skins. (Or cook frozen
baby limas according to package
directions; drain.) Arrange broccoli
flowerets and snow peas in a vegetable
steamer; steam over boiling water 3 to 5
minutes or until broccoli is bright green
but still crisp. Cut snow peas in half.
Put pasta, beans, broccoli, snow peas
and tomatoes in a bowl. Add garlic
vinaigrette and toss together. Transfer
to a serving dish and sprinkle with
oregano. Makes 4 to 5 servings.

Winter Red Salad

1 head oak leaf lettuce or 1 small head
    red leaf lettuce
1 head radicchio
1 red onion, thinly sliced
About 1-1/3 cups shredded red cabbage
About 1 cup diced cooked beets
Walnut Vinaigrette, see below
1/2 pomegranate, peel and pith removed,
    seeds separated

Walnut Vinaigrette:
3 tablespoons walnut oil
1-1/2 tablespoons virgin olive oil
1-1/2 tablespoons red wine vinegar
3/4 teaspoon Dijon-style mustard
Pinch of sugar
Salt and black pepper to taste

Tear large lettuce and radicchio leaves into smaller pieces. Arrange lettuce and radicchio in a bowl. Add onion, cabbage and beets. To prepare Walnut Vinaigrette, stir together all vinaigrette ingredients. Pour vinaigrette over salad and toss. Sprinkle with pomegranate seeds and serve. Makes 4 to 6 servings.

Winter Green Salad

2 cups fresh broccoli flowerets
1 head iceberg lettuce
1 bunch watercress, trimmed
1 (about 15-oz.) can artichoke hearts in
    water, drained, halved
1 fennel bulb, trimmed, thinly sliced
1 green bell pepper, seeded, sliced
Green Goddess Dressing, see below

Green Goddess Dressing:
2/3 cup mayonnaise
2 flat anchovy fillets, drained, finely
    chopped
3 small green onions, finely chopped
2 tablespoons chopped parsley
1 tablespoon tarragon vinegar
1 tablespoon lemon juice
1 garlic clove, crushed
3 tablespoons dairy sour cream
Salt and black pepper to taste

Cook broccoli flowerets in boiling water about 5 minutes or just until bright green and tender-crisp. Drain; let cool. Break lettuce into bite-size pieces and place in a serving bowl along with watercress. Add cooled broccoli, artichokes, fennel and bell pepper. Toss to mix. To prepare Green Goddess Dressing, mix all dressing ingredients (or process in a blender) until well blended. Spoon a little of the dressing over the salad; offer the rest separately. Makes 6 to 8 servings.

Coconut Lime Dressing

2 ozs. creamed coconut
2 tablespoons boiling water
1 teaspoon grated gingerroot
2 teaspoons finely grated lime peel
1 tablespoon fresh lime juice
1 teaspoon honey
1/4 cup plain yogurt

In a small bowl, cover coconut with boiling water. Stir until smooth. Cover and refrigerate until cold. Stir in gingerroot, lime peel and juice, honey and yogurt until well blended. Cover with plastic wrap and refrigerate until needed. Makes 2/3 cup.

Variation: Substitute lemon, orange or grapefruit peel and juice for lime peel and juice.

Note: Use to toss mixed fresh fruit salad or onion and potato salad.

Orange & Sesame Seed Dressing

1 teaspoon tarragon and thyme mustard
1/4 teaspoon salt
1/2 teaspoon black pepper
1 teaspoon finely grated orange peel
1/2 cup sesame oil
2 tablespoons fresh orange juice
1 tablespoon sesame seeds
1 tablespoon chopped fresh tarragon
2 teaspoons chopped fresh thyme

In a small bowl, whisk mustard, salt, pepper, orange peel and sesame oil until well blended. Whisk in orange juice and sesame seeds until mixture becomes cloudy and slightly thick. Cover with plastic wrap and refrigerate until needed. Just before serving, stir in chopped herbs. Makes 2/3 cup.

Variations: Substitute lemon, lime or grapefruit peel and juice for orange peel and juice.

Note: Serve with bitter leaf salad such as endive, radicchio and watercress.

Asparagus with Avocado Dressing

1 lb. fresh asparagus spears
1 ripe avocado
1 tablespoon plus 1 teaspoon chopped
    pistachio nuts or walnuts
Fresh fennel sprigs and orange segments
    to garnish

Marinade:
1/2 cup walnut oil
2 tablespoons fresh orange juice
2 teaspoons grated orange peel
2 teaspoons light-brown sugar
1/2 teaspoon salt
1/2 teaspoon black pepper
2 teaspoons Dijon-style mustard
2 tablespoons chopped fresh fennel

Trim asparagus. Using a sharp knife, peel each stem. In large shallow pan cook asparagus in boiling salted water 5 to 8 minutes or until tender. Drain and cool. To prepare marinade, in a small bowl, combine all marinade ingredients until well blended. Place asparagus in a shallow dish. Pour over marinade, turning asparagus in marinade to coat evenly. Cover and refrigerate 1 hour or until ready to serve. Arrange asparagus on 4 individiual serving plates. Peel and dice avocado. Carefully stir avocado and nuts into marinade. Spoon avocado and nut mixture over center of asparagus. Garnish with fennel, and orange segments. Makes 4 servings.

Dill Cucumber Frais

1 medium-size cucumber
2/3 cup water
1 cup dairy sour cream
Fresh dill sprigs and chive flowers to
    garnish

Marinade:
1 tablespoon plus 1 teaspoon chopped
    fresh tarragon
1 tablespoon plus 1 teaspoon chopped
    fresh dill
1 tablespoon plus 1 teaspoon snipped
    fresh chives
1/2 teaspoon salt
1/2 teaspoon black pepper
1/2 teaspoon dry mustard powder
2 tablespoon red vermouth

Using a zester, remove thin strips of cucumber peel to make a ridge effect. Cut cucumber in half lengthwise. Scoop out seeds and cut in 1/2-inch slices. Bring water to a boil in medium-size saucepan. Cook cucumber 1 minute and drain. To prepare marinade, in a medium-size bowl, combine all marinade ingredients until well blended. Add cucumber, turning cucumber gently in marinade to coat. Cover and refrigerate 2 hours. Just before serving, gently stir in sour cream until evenly mixed. Garnish with dill sprigs and chive flowers. Makes 4 servings.

Chow Mein Salad

4 oz. Chinese egg noodles
1/4 lb. Chinese pea pods, trimmed
6 oz. bean sprouts, roots trimmed
6 green onions, chopped
1 red bell pepper, finely sliced
1/4 lb. mushrooms, sliced
1 small head leaf lettuce, shredded

Dressing:
1/4 cup sunflower oil
2 tablespoons lemon juice
1 tablespoon soy sauce
1 (1-inch) piece ginger root, cut in very thin
    strips

2 tablespoons sesame seed

Bring a medium-size saucepan of salted water to
a boil, break up egg noodles and plunge them
into the water. Boil 5 to 6 minutes or until
tender. Drain and allow noodles to cool.

Split pea pods in half and place in a medium-size
bowl. Pour boiling water over the pea pods and
let stand 2 minutes; drain and cool. Put noodles
and pea pods into a salad bowl with remaining
salad ingredients.

Mix together all ingredients for dressing, pour
over salad and toss together. Sprinkle with
sesame seed. Makes 6 to 8 servings.

Summer Vegetable Salad

3/4 lb. eggplant, diced
3 tablespoons olive oil
1 medium-size yellow onion, sliced
3/4 lb. zucchini, sliced
1 red bell pepper, cut in chunks
1 green bell pepper, cut in chunks
1 yellow bell pepper, cut in chunks
3 tomatoes, skinned, chopped
1 tablespoon chopped fresh basil
Salt and pepper
1 tablespoon chopped fresh parsley (optional)

Put eggplant in a colander, sprinkle with salt and
let stand 30 minutes to drain. Rinse and dry.

Heat oil in a large skillet, add eggplant and
onion and cook over medium heat 5 minutes.
Add zucchini and peppers and cook over low
heat 15 minutes, turning them over until tender.

Transfer vegetables to a large serving bowl. Stir
in tomatoes, basil, salt and pepper; let cool.
Chill before serving. Sprinkle with chopped
parsley. Makes 6 to 8 servings.

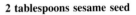

Potato Salad

1-1/2 lbs. new potatoes, scrubbed
6 green onions, chopped
1 tablespoon chopped fresh parsley
1 teaspoon chopped fresh marjoram
1 tablespoon chopped fresh dill

Yogurt Dressing:
5 tablespoons plain low-fat yogurt
3 tablespoons mayonnaise
2 teaspoons lemon juice
1 teaspoon Dijon mustard
Salt and pepper

Cook potatoes in boiling salted water until tender; drain and allow to cool. Cut potatoes in thick slices and put in a serving bowl. Reserve some chopped green onions and herbs for garnishing then add remainder to potatoes; toss together.

Blend together all ingredients for Yogurt Dressing and pour over potatoes; chill. Mix lightly, garnish with reserved green onions and herbs and serve. Makes about 6 servings.

Mixed Leaf Salad

1/2 head romaine lettuce, shredded
1/2 head iceberg lettuce, shredded
1 medium-size avocado
2 teaspoons lemon juice
1 green bell pepper, sliced
1/2 cucumber, sliced
6 green onions, chopped
Watercress, trimmed
Curly endive
3 celery stalks, chopped

Dressing:
2 tablespoons walnut oil
2 tablespoons sunflower oil
1 tablespoon white-wine vinegar
1/2 teaspoon Dijon mustard
Salt and pepper

Put lettuce in a large salad bowl. Cut avocado in half, remove seed and peel. Cut in slices and coat with lemon juice. Add avocado slices and remaining salad ingredients to lettuce in bowl.

Mix all ingredients for dressing together, pour over salad and toss together. Makes about 6 to 8 servings.

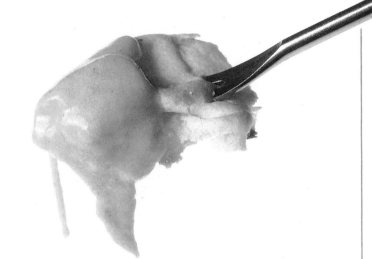

Classic Swiss Fondue

1 garlic clove, halved
1 cup dry white wine
1 teaspoon lemon juice
2 cups (8 oz.) shredded Gruyère cheese
2 cups (8 oz.) shredded Emmentaler cheese
2 teaspoons cornstarch
2 tablespoons kirsch
Dash white pepper
Pinch grated nutmeg

To Serve:
French bread, cut in cubes

Rub inside of fondue pot with cut garlic clove.

Pour in wine and lemon juice; cook over medium heat until bubbly. Turn heat to low and gradually stir in cheeses with a wooden spoon.

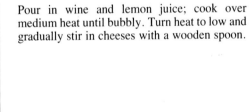

In a small bowl blend cornstarch with kirsch. Blend into cheese and continue to cook, stirring, 2 to 3 minutes or until mixture is thick and smooth. Do not allow fondue to boil. Season with white pepper and nutmeg. Serve with bread cubes. Makes about 4 servings.

Curried Cheese Fondue

1 garlic clove, halved
2/3 cup dry white wine
1 teaspoon lemon juice
2 teaspoons curry paste
8 oz. process Gruyère cheese
8 oz. Cheddar cheese
1 teaspoon cornstarch
2 tablespoons dry sherry

To Serve:
pita bread rounds, cut in pieces

Shred cheeses.

Rub inside of fondue pot with cut garlic clove. Pour in wine and lemon juice; cook over medium heat until bubbly. Turn heat to low and add curry paste. Gradually stir in shredded cheeses.

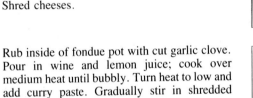

In a small bowl blend cornstarch with sherry. Blend into cheese and continue to cook, stirring, 2 to 3 minutes or until mixture is thick and smooth. Do not allow fondue to boil. Serve with pieces of pita bread rounds. Makes 4 to 6 servings.

Somerset Fondue

1 small onion, halved
1 cup apple cider
1 teaspoon lemon juice
3 cups (12 oz.) shredded Cheddar cheese
1/2 teaspoon dry mustard
1 tablespoon cornstarch
3 tablespoons apple juice
Dash white pepper

To Serve:
wedges of apple, cubes of bread

Rub inside of fondue pot with cut side of onion.

Pour in cider and lemon juice; cook over medium heat until bubbly. Turn heat to low and gradually stir in cheese. Continue to heat until cheese melts.

In a small bowl blend mustard and cornstarch with apple juice. Blend into cheese and continue to cook, stirring, 2 to 3 minutes or until mixture is thick and creamy. Season with white pepper. Serve with apple wedges and cubes of crusty bread. Makes about 6 servings.

Dutch Fondue

1 small onion, halved
1 cup milk
4 cups (1 lb.) shredded Gouda cheese
2 teaspoons caraway seeds
1 tablespoon cornstarch
3 tablespoons gin
Pepper

To Serve:
mushrooms, cubes of light rye bread

Measure ingredients. Rub inside of fondue pot with cut side of onion.

Add milk and heat until bubbly; then gradually stir in cheese. Continue to heat until cheese melts.

Stir in caraway seeds. In a small bowl blend cornstarch with gin. Blend into cheese mixture and cook, stirring, 2 to 3 minutes or until smooth and creamy. Season with pepper. Serve with mushrooms and light rye bread. Makes 4 to 6 servings.

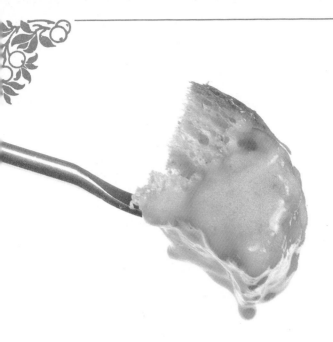

Pub Fondue

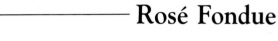

Rosé Fondue

1 garlic clove, halved
1-1/4 cups beer
2 cups (8 oz.) shredded Leicester or mild
   Cheddar cheese
2 cups (8 oz.) shredded sharp Cheddar cheese
1 tablespoon all-purpose flour
1 teaspoon dry mustard
Pepper

To Serve:
cubes of whole-wheat bread, pickles

Rub inside of fondue pot with cut garlic clove.
Add beer and heat until bubbly.

Toss cheeses in flour and mustard.

Over low heat add cheeses to beer. Season with
pepper and continue to heat, stirring constantly,
until mixture is smooth. Serve with whole-
wheat bread cubes and pickles. Makes 4 to 6
servings.

1 garlic clove, halved
1 cup rosé wine
1 cup (4 oz.) shredded Gruyère cheese
2 cups (8 oz.) shredded Cheddar cheese with
   wine
1 tablespoon cornstarch
2 tablespoons kirsch

To Serve:
French bread, cut in cubes

Rub inside of fondue pot with cut garlic clove.
Add wine and heat until bubbly.

Gradually stir in cheeses and continue to cook
over medium heat until melted.

In a small bowl mix cornstarch with kirsch;
blend into cheese mixture. Cook, stirring, 2 to 3
minutes or until smooth and thickened. Serve
with cubes of French bread. Makes about 6
servings.

Beer Fondue

1 tablespoon butter
1 small onion, chopped
1 cup light ale
4 cups (1 lb.) shredded Lancashire or Monterey
  Jack cheese
4 teaspoons cornstarch
5 tablespoons half and half

To Serve:
cauliflower florets, radishes and mushrooms

Melt butter in a large saucepan and cook onion until soft. Pour in ale and heat until bubbly.

Over low heat, stir in cheese. Continue to heat until cheese has melted.

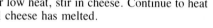

In a small bowl blend cornstarch with half and half. Add to cheese mixture and cook, stirring, 2 to 3 minutes or until smooth and thickened. Serve with cauliflower florets, radishes and mushrooms. Makes 4 to 6 servings.

Normandy Fondue

1 garlic clove, halved
1/2 cup dry white wine
2/3 cup half and half
12 oz. Camembert cheese, rind removed
1 tablespoon cornstarch
1/4 cup calvados brandy

To Serve:
French bread, chunks of apple

Rub inside of fondue pot with cut garlic clove. Add wine and half and half; heat until bubbly.

Cut cheese in small pieces and add to wine mixture. Stir over low heat until melted.

In a small bowl blend cornstarch with calvados; add to cheese mixture. Continue to cook, stirring 2 to 3 minutes or until thick and creamy. Serve with cubes of French bread and chunks of apple. Makes about 6 servings.

Highland Fondue

1 small onion, chopped
1 tablespoon butter
1 cup milk
4 cups (1 lb.) shredded Cheddar cheese
1 tablespoon cornstarch
1/4 cup whisky

To Serve:
cubes of rye and onion breads

In a medium-size saucepan cook onion in butter over low heat until soft. Add milk and heat until bubbly.

Gradually stir in cheese and continue to cook until melted.

In a small bowl blend cornstarch with whisky; stir into cheese mixture. Cook, stirring, 2 to 3 minutes or until thickened. Pour into fondue pot and serve with cubes of rye and onion breads. Makes 4 to 6 servings.

Welsh Fondue

2 tablespoons butter
1/2 lb. leeks, trimmed and finely chopped
2 tablespoons all-purpose flour
1 cup beer
2-1/2 cups (10 oz.) shredded Caerphilly cheese
Pepper

To Serve:
cubes of French bread

In a large saucepan melt butter over low heat. Add leeks, cover pan and cook 10 minutes or until tender.

Stir in flour and cook 1 minute. Add beer and heat, stirring constantly, until thickened.

Gradually add cheese and continue to cook, stirring, until cheese melts. Season with pepper. Pour into fondue pot and serve with cubes of French bread. Makes 4 to 6 servings.

Vegetable Samosa

8 ounces potatoes, cut in even-size pieces
3/4 cup frozen green peas
2 tablespoons corn oil
1 onion, finely chopped
1/2 teaspoon cumin seeds
1 (1/2-inch) piece ginger root, peeled, grated
1/2 teaspoon tumeric
1/2 teaspoon garam masala
1/2 teaspoon salt
2 teaspoons lemon juice
1 cup all-purpose flour
2 tablespoons butter
2 tablespoons warm milk
Vegetable oil for deep frying
Lime twists, if desired
Fresh celery leaves, if desired
Mango chutney

In a saucepan, boil potatoes in salted water 15 to 20 minutes or until tender. Drain well, return to saucepan and shake over low heat a few moments or until dry. Mash well. Cook peas in boiling salted water 4 minutes. Drain well.

Heat oil in a skillet. Add onion, cumin seeds, ginger, turmeric, garam masala and salt. Cook gently 5 minutes. Add mashed potatoes and peas, then stir in lemon juice. Mix well, remove from heat and cool.

Sift flour into a bowl. Cut in butter finely until mixture resembles bread crumbs. Add milk and mix to form a stiff dough. Divide in 6 equal pieces.

Form each piece in a ball and roll each ball on a lightly floured surface to a 6-inch circle. Cut each circle in half. Divide filling equally among semicircles of pastry.

Dampen edges of pastry, then fold over and seal to form triangles which enclose filling completely. Half fill a deep-fat fryer or saucepan with oil. Heat oil to 375F (190C) or until a 1/2-inch cube of day-old bread browns in 40 seconds. Fry samosa in hot oil, a few at a time, 3 to 4 minutes or until golden brown. Drain on paper towels. Garnish with lime twists and celery leaves, if desired, and serve hot with mango chutney. Makes 12 samosa.

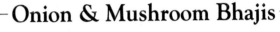

Eggplant Tahini Pâté

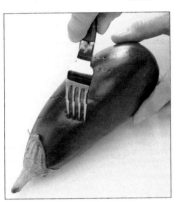

1 large eggplant
1 large clove garlic
3 shallots
1/2 to 1 teaspoon garam masala
3 tablespoons tahini (creamed sesame)
Finely grated peel 1 lemon
3 tablespoons lemon juice
Salt to taste
2 teaspoons olive oil
Cayenne pepper
Lemon slices, if desired, cut in half
Fresh parsley sprig, if desired
Pita bread, cut in strips

Preheat oven to 350F (175C). Prick eggplant several times with a fork.

Bake eggplant in preheated oven 30 to 40 minutes or until softened and skin has turned dark brown. Cool, trim ends and peel eggplant. Process flesh in a blender or food processor with garlic, shallots, garam masala, tahini, lemon peel and juice until smooth and evenly combined.

Season with salt. Spoon mixture into a serving bowl, drizzle with olive oil and sprinkle with cayenne pepper. Garnish with lemon slices and parsley sprig, if desired, and serve with pita bread. Makes 4 to 6 servings.

Onion & Mushroom Bhajis

1 onion
2 ounces button mushrooms
1/4 cup brown rice flour
1/4 cup all-purpose flour
1/2 teaspoon turmeric
1/2 teaspoon hot chili powder
1/4 teaspoon ground cumin
1/4 teaspoon ground coriander
1/4 teaspoon salt
2/3 cup plain yogurt
Vegetable oil for deep frying
Fresh parsley sprig, if desired

Peel, quarter and thinly slice onion.

Coarsely chop mushrooms. In a bowl, combine flours, turmeric, chili powder, cumin, coriander and salt. Stir in onion, mushrooms and yogurt; mix well.

Half fill a deep-fat fryer or saucepan with oil; heat to 375F (190C) or until a 1/2-inch cube of day-old bread browns in 40 seconds. Divide mixture in 10 equal portions. Drop spoonfuls of mixture into hot oil and fry 3 to 4 minutes or until golden brown and cooked through. Drain on paper towels. Garnish with parsley sprig, if desired, and serve warm. Makes 10 appetizers.

Guacamole

2 ripe avocados
1 tablespoon lemon juice
1 small clove garlic, if desired
1 small fresh green chili, seeded
1 shallot, finely chopped
1 tablespoon olive oil
Few drops hot-pepper sauce
Salt to taste
1 lemon slice, cut in pieces
Fresh Italian parsley sprig, if desired
Tortilla chips

Cut avocados in half, remove seeds and scoop flesh onto a plate. Mash well.

Add lemon juice and garlic, if desired, and mix well. Very finely chop chili and add to mixture with shallot.

Stir in olive oil, hot-pepper sauce and salt and mix well. Spoon mixture into a serving bowl and garnish with lemon pieces and parsley sprig, if desired. Serve with tortilla chips. Makes 4 to 6 servings.

Spanakopita

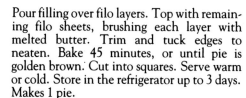

1 lb. fresh spinach, washed, and stems removed
1/2 lb. feta cheese
2 tablespoons finely chopped shallots
2 onions, thinly sliced
1 tablespoon finely chopped thyme
1 tablespoon finely chopped rosemary
2 tablespoons finely chopped oregano
2 tablespoons finely chopped fennel
6 eggs
1/2 cup vegetable oil
1 teaspoon salt
Fresh ground pepper
14 sheets filo pastry
3/4 cup butter, melted

Preheat oven to 350F (175C). Steam spinach leaves until limp. Cool; squeeze out all moisture. Combine spinach with cheese, shallots, onion and herbs. Set aside. In separate bowl, beat together eggs, oil, salt and pepper. Stir egg mixture into spinach mixture.

Brush a 13 × 9-inch baking pan with a little of the melted butter. Lay a sheet of filo on pan and brush lightly with butter. Repeat using 6 more sheets.

Pour filling over filo layers. Top with remaining filo sheets, brushing each layer with melted butter. Trim and tuck edges to neaten. Bake 45 minutes, or until pie is golden brown. Cut into squares. Serve warm or cold. Store in the refrigerator up to 3 days. Makes 1 pie.

Potato Skins with Sour Cream

Pears Stuffed with Gorgonzola

3 lbs. medium-size russet potatoes
5 tablespoons butter, melted
Salt
2/3 cup sour cream
2 tablespoons snipped chives

Preheat oven to 400F (205C). Scrub potatoes and prick with a fork; place in an ovenproof dish. Bake about 1 hour until tender.

8 small ripe pears, peeled
Juice of 3 lemons, in a large bowl
1/4 lb. Gorgonzola cheese, softened
1/4 cup butter, softened
1/4 cup finely chopped walnuts or pistachio nuts

Slice pears in half, taking care to leave stem intact on one half. Core pears using a spoon, remove a tablespoon of the flesh to form a hollow. Immediately immerse pears in bowl with lemon juice to prevent discoloration.

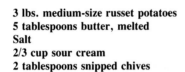

Remove potatoes from oven and cut each in quarters. Remove insides leaving about 1/4-inch flesh on inside of skins. (The cooked potato can be used in soups.) Increase oven temperature to 450F (230C).

In a small bowl, beat together cheese and butter until smooth. Fill each pear half with about a tablespoon of mixture.

Brush inside and outside of each potato skin with butter, sprinkle with salt and place on a baking sheet. Bake about 10 minutes or until crisp. Mix sour cream with chives and serve with the cooked potato skins. Makes about 6 servings.

Press pears together and roll in walnuts. Refrigerate at least 2 hours. Serve as first course. Store in the refrigerator up to 3 days. Makes 8 servings.

Blue Cheese Dip and Crackers

BLUE CHEESE DIP:
1-1/2 cups blue cheese, chopped
1 cup drained crushed pineapple
1/2 cup sour cream
1/2 cup cottage cheese
2 tablespoons fresh chopped chives
Chive sprigs, finely chopped chives, radish slices
  for decoration

In a food processor or blender, blend all ingredients, except chive sprigs.

When just combined, pour into bowl or bowls.

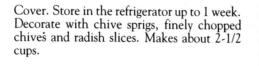

Cover. Store in the refrigerator up to 1 week. Decorate with chive sprigs, finely chopped chives and radish slices. Makes about 2-1/2 cups.

CHEDDAR CHEESE CRACKERS:
2/3 cup wholewheat flour
2 tablespoons self-raising flour
1/2 teaspoon salt
1/4 teaspoon cayenne pepper
1/2 cup butter
1/2 cup grated Cheddar cheese
1 tablespoon lemon juice
1 egg

Preheat oven to 325F (160C). In food processor or blender, combine all ingredients. Blend until dough is formed. Shape mixture into a roll 15 inches long. Wrap in plastic wrap. Refrigerate at least 3 hours. Cut roll into slices 1/4-inch thick, place on lightly greased cookie sheets. Bake 15 minutes. Cool. Makes about 60.

BRAN CRACKERS:
1/2 cup unprocessed bran
3/4 cup wholewheat flour
1 tablespoon packed brown sugar
1/2 cup butter
2 eggs
Pinch of salt

Preheat oven to 325F (160C). In food processor or blender, combine bran, wholewheat flour, sugar and butter. Blend until butter is completely cut into flour mixture. Add eggs and salt. Blend until dough forms. Turn mixture out onto a floured board and knead lightly. Divide dough in half. Press each half into greased 11 × 7-inch baking pan. Prick surface with fork. Bake 15 minutes. Cut into squares. Cool. Makes about 35.

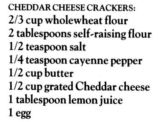

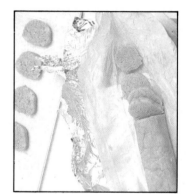

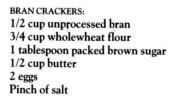

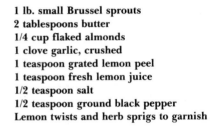

Broccoli & Cauliflower Crumble

8 oz. cauliflower florets
8 oz. broccoli florets
Hard-cooked egg wedges and parsley sprigs to
 garnish

Topping:
2 tablespoons butter
1 cup soft white bread crumbs
1 tablespoon chopped fresh parsley
1 hard-cooked egg, sieved

Sauce:
2 tablespoons butter
1/4 cup all-purpose flour
1-1/4 cups milk
1/2 teaspoon salt
1/2 teaspoon ground black pepper

To prepare topping, heat butter in a skillet. Add bread crumbs and fry until golden brown and crisp. In a bowl, combine bread crumbs, parsley and sieved egg.

To prepare sauce, place butter, flour, milk, salt and pepper in a saucepan. Whisk over moderate heat until thick. Cook 1 to 2 minutes. Keep warm.

In a saucepan, cook cauliflower and broccoli in boiling salted water 3 to 4 minutes or until just tender. Drain and place in a warmed serving dish. Pour over sauce and sprinkle with topping. Garnish with egg wedges and parsley sprigs. Makes 4 to 6 servings.

Brussel Sprouts with Almonds

1 lb. small Brussel sprouts
2 tablespoons butter
1/4 cup flaked almonds
1 clove garlic, crushed
1 teaspoon grated lemon peel
1 teaspoon fresh lemon juice
1/2 teaspoon salt
1/2 teaspoon ground black pepper
Lemon twists and herb sprigs to garnish

Trim tops off sprouts and cut across top of each. In a saucepan, cook sprouts in boiling salted water 4 to 5 minutes or until just tender. Drain well and place in a warmed serving dish.

Meanwhile, melt butter in a skillet. Add flaked almonds and garlic. Fry until almonds are golden brown. Stir in lemon peel, juice, salt and pepper and mix well.

Sprinkle almonds over sprouts; stir gently to mix. Garnish with lemon twists and herb sprigs. Makes 4 servings.

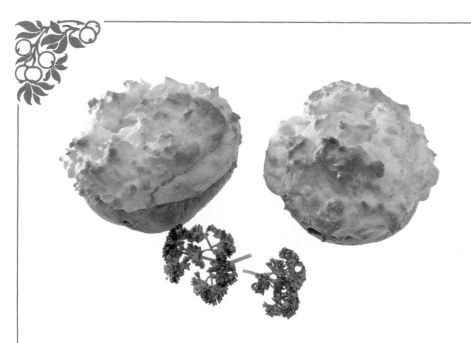

Soufflé Potatoes

4 large potatoes
2 tablespoons butter
2 tablespoons half and half
1 teaspoon salt
1/2 teaspoon ground black pepper
1/2 teaspoon grated nutmeg
2 eggs, separated
Parsley sprigs to garnish

Preheat oven to 425F (220C). Scrub potatoes until skins are clean and remove any 'eyes.' Using a small sharp knife, pierce each potato several times and arrange on a baking sheet. Bake in oven 1 hour or until potatoes are tender.

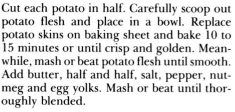

Cut each potato in half. Carefully scoop out potato flesh and place in a bowl. Replace potato skins on baking sheet and bake 10 to 15 minutes or until crisp and golden. Meanwhile, mash or beat potato flesh until smooth. Add butter, half and half, salt, pepper, nutmeg and egg yolks. Mash or beat until thoroughly blended.

In a small bowl, stiffly whisk egg whites until stiff. Using a spatula, gently fold egg whites into potato mixture until evenly mixed. Fill each potato skin with mixture and bake 10 to 15 minutes or until risen and lightly browned. Garnish with parsley sprigs and serve immediately. Makes 8 servings.

Variation:
Add 1/2 cup chopped crispy bacon, shredded cheese or chopped mixed fresh herbs to potato mixture.

Creamed Spinach & Celery

2 lb. fresh spinach
6 stalks celery
2 tablespoons butter
1 teaspoon grated nutmeg
1/3 cup whipping cream
1/4 teaspoon salt
1/2 teaspoon ground black pepper
Additional celery slices and leaves to garnish

Stem and wash spinach. Wash and thinly slice celery. In 2 saucepans, cook celery and spinach separately in boiling salted water until just tender. Drain thoroughly. Press excess water from spinach.

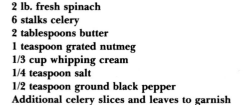

Line bottom and sides of 8 warm individual soufflé dishes with whole spinach leaves. Coarsely chop remaining spinach. Melt butter in a saucepan. Add nutmeg, whipping cream, salt and pepper and bring to a boil. Add chopped spinach and toss well.

Half-fill each soufflé dish with spinach mixture and cover each with a layer of celery. Fill each to top with remaining chopped spinach. Press firmly. Invert spinach molds to serve. Garnish with celery slices and leaves. Makes 8 servings.

Baked Potato Layer

2 lb. medium-size potatoes
2 tablespoons butter
1 clove garlic, crushed
1 teaspoon salt
1 teaspoon ground black pepper
1 cup shredded Cheddar cheese (4 oz.)
1-1/4 cups milk
2/3 cup half and half
1 large egg, beaten
Parsley sprigs to garnish

Preheat oven to 375F (190C). Using a sharp knife, peel and very thinly slice potatoes or use a food processor fitted with a fine slicing blade. Lightly butter a 9-inch shallow oven-proof dish using 1/2 of butter.

Arrange a layer of potato slices over bottom and up sides of dish. Sprinkle with some of garlic, salt, pepper and cheese. Continue to layer until all these ingredients have been used, finishing with a layer of potatoes and a sprinkling of cheese.

In a bowl, whisk milk, half and half and egg until smooth. Pour over potato layer and dot with remaining butter. Bake 1 hour or until golden brown and potatoes are tender. Garnish with parsley sprigs and serve hot. Makes 4 servings.

Glazed Carrots & Onions

12 small even-sized carrots
16 pickling onions
1 teaspoon salt
1/4 cup turkey or chicken stock
1 tablespoon superfine sugar
2 tablespoons butter
1 tablespoon chopped fresh parsley
Herb sprigs to garnish

Peel and trim carrots so they are all even in size. Peel and trim onions. In 2 saucepans, cook carrots and onions separately in boiling salted water 5 to 8 minutes or until just tender. Drain well.

In a medium saucepan, combine stock, sugar and butter. Heat gently, stirring until sugar has dissolved and butter has melted. Boil rapidly until mixture is reduced by half.

Add carrots, onions and parsley. Toss well in glaze and arrange on a warmed serving dish. Garnish with herb sprigs. Makes 4 servings.

— Spicy Sesame Noodles —

2 tablespoons sesame seeds
1 tablespoon sesame oil
4 teaspoons peanut butter
2 tablespoon soy sauce
2 teaspoons chili sauce
1/2 teaspoon sugar
1/4 cup water
8 oz. rice vermicelli
Carrot blossoms, if desired
Toasted sesame seeds, if desired

In a 6-inch skillet, brown sesame seeds over medium heat. Crush slightly. In a bowl or food processor, mix together browned sesame seeds, sesame oil, peanut butter, soy sauce, chili sauce, sugar and water. Set aside. Put vermicelli into a medium-size bowl. Cover with boiling water. Soak 10 minutes. Drain thoroughly. Put drained vermicelli and sesame sauce in a 2-1/2-quart saucepan. Mix together to coat vermicelli in sauce. Cook over low heat until thoroughly heated through. Garnish with carrot blossoms and sesame seeds, if desired. Makes 4 servings.

— Buckwheat Noodles with Eggs —

12 oz. buckwheat noodles
2 tablespoons vegetable oil
1 onion, chopped
4 cups shredded Chinese
  cabbage (6 oz.)
4 eggs, beaten
Salt and pepper
1 tablespoon soy sauce
Fresh bay leaf, if desired
Lemon peel rose, if desired

In a large saucepan of boiling salted water, cook noodles in the same way as spaghetti until tender. Drain. Meanwhile, in a large saucepan, heat oil. Add onion; cook until soft. Add Chinese cabbage; cook until beginning to soften. Stir in eggs. Cook, stirring, about 1 minute or until eggs are beginning to set. Stir drained noodles into egg mixture. Add salt, pepper and soy sauce. Garnish with bay leaf and lemon peel rose, if desired, and serve at once. Makes 4 servings.

Eggplant Filled Mushrooms with Basil

8 large mushrooms
1 eggplant
1 garlic clove, crushed
1 (3-oz.) pkg. cream cheese
Salt and black pepper to taste
Fresh basil sprigs to garnish

Marinade:
3 tomatoes, peeled, seeded
1/4 cup olive oil
1/4 teaspoon salt
1/4 teaspoon black pepper
1 teaspoon sugar
Juice 1 orange
1 tablespoon plus 1 teaspoon chopped
    fresh basil

Remove stalks from mushrooms. To prepare marinade, in a food processor fitted with a metal blade, process stalks and all marinade ingredients until smooth. Spoon marinade into each mushroom and pour remainder into a small dish. Cover and refrigerate 1 hour. Meanwhile, preheat oven to 425F (220C). Bake eggplant in pre-heated oven 15 to 20 minutes or until skin is charred and flesh is tender. Cool and peel. Scrape out flesh into food processor fitted with a metal blade. Add garlic and cream cheese. Season to taste with salt and pepper. Process mixture until smooth. Place mushrooms on a baking sheet. Bake 5 minutes. Spoon eggplant mixture into each mushroom. Return to oven 5 to 8 minutes or until filling has set and mushrooms are tender. Garnish with basil sprigs. Makes 4 servings.

Crispy Coated Vegetables

8 large mushrooms, cut in half
2 zucchini, cut in 1/2-inch slices
1 cup Chinese snow peas or dwarf
    French green beans, ends removed
1 small fennel bulb, broken in bite-size
    pieces
1 cup cauliflower or broccoli floweretes
1 cup self-rising flour
1 egg
2/3 cup water
Oil for deep-frying
Lime wedges and fresh fennel sprigs to
    garnish

Marinade:
2 tablespoons plus 2 teaspoons chopped
    fresh basil
2 teaspoons finely grated lime peel
1 tablespoon fresh lime juice
1 teaspoon finely grated gingerroot
1 teaspoon superfine sugar
2 tablespoons olive oil
1/2 teaspoon salt
1/2 teaspoon black pepper

To prepare marinade, in a large bowl, combine all marinade ingredients until well blended. Add all vegetables to marinade, turning vegetables in mari-nade to coat evenly. Cover and refriger-ate 1 hour or until ready to cook. To prepare batter, place flour in a medi-um-size bowl. Make a "well" in center. Add egg yolk and gradually stir in water. Beat until smooth. Stiffly whisk egg white and fold into batter just be-fore using. Half-fill a deep saucepan with oil. Heat to 350F (175C). Dip 1 piece of vegetable at a time into batter to coat evenly, then place in oil. Fry about 12 pieces of vegetables at a time until lightly browned and crisp. Drain on paper towels. Garnish with lime and fennel sprigs. Makes 4 servings.

Egg & Mushroom Benedict

2 English muffins
1/2 cup herb butter, see Note
4 large shiitake or mushrooms
4 eggs plus 1 extra egg yolk
2 tablespoons white wine vinegar
1 tablespoon water
8 tablespoons butter, melted
Salt and pepper to taste
Sprigs of chervil to garnish

Split muffins in half and toast on both sides. Preheat broiler. In a small saucepan, melt herb butter and generously brush both sides of each mushroom. Broil 2 minutes on each side. Bring a large pan of water to simmering point and carefully crack 4 eggs into water. Poach 3 to 4 minutes, then remove with a slotted spoon and drain on paper towels. In a small saucepan, bring vinegar and water to a boil and reduce by half. In a blender or food processor fitted with the metal blade, process egg yolk 30 seconds, pouring in hot vinegar reduction; slowly add melted butter. Season with salt and pepper. Place a mushroom on top of each muffin half, top with a poached egg and spoon sauce over egg. Garnish with sprigs of chervil and serve immediately.

Makes 4 servings.

Note: To prepare herb butter, mix 1 tablespoon of finely chopped fresh herbs and 1/2 cup of softened butter.

Cheesy Bread

3 cups self-rising flour
1 teaspoon baking powder
1/4 teaspoon salt
1 teaspoon sugar
1 cup milk
2 teaspoons prepared mustard
1/2 cup shredded Cheddar cheese (2 oz.)
1/2 cup shredded Gloucester cheese with
    chives (2 oz.)
4 tablespoons butter, softened
2 tablespoons half and half
2 teaspoons dry sherry
2 teaspoons chpped fresh chives

Preheat oven to 425F (220C). Dust a baking sheet with flour. Sift flour, baking powder, salt and sugar into a large bowl. In a glass measure, combine milk and mustard and pour into dry ingredients. Mix quickley to form a soft dough. Place dough on prepared baking sheet. Press out to a circle about 1-1/2 inches thick. Using a sharp knife, mark in 8 wedges. Sprinkle with Cheddar cheese and bake in preheated oven 10 minutes. Lower oven temperature to 400F (205C) and bake 20 minutes more, until well risen and golden. Cool slightly. In a blender or a food processor fitted with the metal blade, process double Gloucester cheese, butter, half and half, sherry and chives until mixed. Spoon into a serving dish and serve with hot bread.

Makes 8 servings.

Herb Popovers with Buttered Eggs

Herb Popovers:
3/4 cup all-purpose flour
1/2 teaspoon celery salt
2 large eggs
1 cup milk
1 tablespoon butter, melted
2 tablespoons chopped fresh mixed herbs,
   such as chervil, parsley, chives and
   tarragon

Buttered Eggs:
1/4 cup butter
6 large eggs, beaten
2 tablespoons chopped fresh mixed herbs,
   such as chervil, parsley, chives and
   tarragon
2 tablespoons half and half
Salt and pepper to taste

To prepare popovers, generously grease a 12-cup muffin pan. Sift flour and celery salt into a large bowl. Add eggs, milk and butter and beat well. Stir in mixed herbs. Pour mixture into greased muffin cups. Place in cold oven, set temperature at 425F (220C) and bake 30 minutes without opening oven door. To prepare buttered eggs, melt butter in a small saucepan. Add eggs and cook over low heat, stirring constantly, until thickened. Remove from heat and stir in mixed herbs and half and half. Season with salt and pepper. Serve each person 2 popovers with a mound of buttered eggs.

Makes 6 servings.

Avocado & Camembert Omelet

4 large eggs
2 tablespoons grated Parmesan cheese
2 tablespoons butter
1 small avocado
1 tablespoon dairy sour cream
Pinch of ground nutmeg
Salt and pepper to taste
2 ounces Camembert cheese, diced
Sprigs of parsley to garnish

In a large bowl, beat eggs and Parmesan cheese. In a large skillet, melt 1/2 of butter and pour in 1/2 of egg mixture. Cook until set. Prepare remaining omelet in same way. Cut avocado in half and discard pit. Slice 1 avocado half thinly in long fingers. In a small bowl, mash remaining half. Stir in sour cream and nutmeg. Season with salt and pepper. Stir in camembert cheese. Arrange 1/2 of avocado fingers in a fan shape on top of each omelet and top each with 1/2 of camembert mixture. Broil 1 minute, until cheese melts. Fold omelets in half and place on warmed plates. Garnish with sprigs of parsley and serve immediately.

Makes 2 servings.

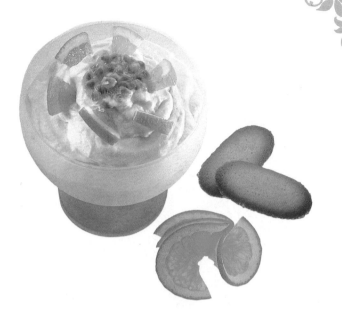

Crème Brûlée

Tropical Flummery

4 egg yolks
2-1/2 teaspoons superfine sugar
Pinch of cornstarch
2-1/2 cups whipping cream
2 vanilla beans
Additional superfine sugar
Frosted flowers to serve, if desired

In a large bowl, beat egg yolks, sugar and cornstarch lightly.

Pour whipping cream into a saucepan. With a sharp knife, split open vanilla beans and scrape seeds into whipping cream. Bring almost to boiling point, strain and pour over yolks, beating constantly. Pour into top of a double boiler or a bowl set over a pan of simmering water. Cook over medium heat until mixture thickens sufficiently to coat back of a spoon. Pour into individual flameproof gratin dishes. Cool and chill overnight.

Two hours before serving, preheat broiler. Cover surface of pudding thickly and evenly with additional sugar and broil until sugar caramelizes. Chill 2 hours. Serve with frosted flowers, if desired.

Makes 4 to 6 servings.

NOTE: The best vanilla beans are coated in white crystals and are very expensive. All vanilla beans can be washed after use and used again. Store in a dry place.

1-1/4 cups whipping cream
1/3 cup thawed frozen concentrated tropical fruit juice
1 egg white
1 tablespoon plus 2 teaspoons superfine sugar
Orange wedges and passion fruit to decorate, if desired
Langue de chats cookies to serve

In a bowl, whip cream to soft peaks.

Add fruit juice gradually, continuing to whip cream until fairly thick.

In a separate bowl, whisk egg white until stiff. Whisk in sugar, then fold into creamy mixture. Spoon into individual dessert dishes and chill 1 hour. Decorate with orange wedges and passion fruit, if desired. Serve with cookies.

Makes 4 to 6 servings.

NOTE: To flavor sugar for desserts and cakes, keep it in a container with a vanilla bean. This will give it a strong vanilla flavor.

Gooseberry Ice Cream

1-1/2 pounds fresh or frozen gooseberries
1/4 cup water
1/2 cup superfine sugar
3 egg yolks
1 small avocado
1-1/4 cups whipping cream
Gooseberries, fresh herbs or borage flowers to
    decorate, if desired

In a saucepan, combine gooseberries and 2 tablespoons of water. Cook over a low heat until gooseberries are soft. Puree in a blender or food processor, then sieve to remove seeds; cool.

Combine remaining water and sugar in a saucepan. Dissolve over medium heat, stirring constantly, then boil syrup to thread stage 225F (105C). In a bowl, beat egg yolks lightly, then pour syrup into them and whisk until mixture is thick and mousse-like. Peel avocado, discard pit and mash pulp; mix into gooseberry puree. Whip cream and fold into egg mixture with puree. Turn into a rigid plastic container and freeze 1 to 2 hours, until beginning to firm.

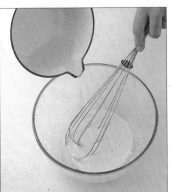

Remove from freezer and beat well. Freeze until firm. Transfer to refrigerator 30 minutes before serving to soften. Serve in scoops in chilled dessert dishes. Decorate with gooseberries, fresh herbs or borage flowers, if desired.

Makes 4 to 6 servings.

NOTE: Avocado gives this ice-cream a lovely texture. Its taste is not discernible.
When cooking acidic fruits, such as gooseberries, do not use an aluminum pan, or the fruit will taste metallic.

Nutty-Crumb Cream

1/2 cup hazelnuts
1-1/4 cups fresh whole-wheat bread crumbs
2 tablespoons light-brown sugar
2 egg whites
1/3 cup superfine sugar
1-1/4 cups whipping cream
1 to 2 drops vanilla extract
Fresh flower buds or leaves to decorate, if
    desired

Toast hazelnuts under broiler evenly. Cool, then grind coarsely in a coffee grinder or a food processor fitted with the metal blade. In a bowl, mix ground nuts with bread crumbs and brown sugar.

Spread crumb mixture evenly on a baking sheet. Broil, turning and shaking, until brown; cool. Whisk egg whites in a large bowl, until stiff. Sprinkle in sugar and whisk 2 minutes more. Whip cream and vanilla to soft peaks, then fold into egg whites with all but 1 tablespoon of browned crumb mixture.

Spoon mixture into 6 dessert dishes and chill until ready to serve. Sprinkle with reserved crumb mixture just before serving. Decorate with fresh flower buds or leaves, if desired.

Makes 6 servings.

NOTE: This mixture makes a delicious ice cream. Pour finished cream into a plastic container and freeze.

Oeufs à la Neige

4 eggs, separated
1/2 teaspoon cornstarch
1/3 cup superfine sugar
1/2 cup milk
1-1/4 cups half and half
1 vanilla bean
1 tablespoon orange flower water
1 tablespoon toasted whole almonds and orange
    peel strips to decorate, if desired

In a bowl, cream egg yolks, cornstarch and 1/2 of sugar. In a saucepan, scald milk, half and half and vanilla bean.

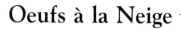

Pour hot milk over egg yolks, whisking constantly. Pour egg mixture back into pan; set over a pan of simmering water and cook gently, stirring constantly, until consistency of thick cream. Cool, remove vanilla bean and stir in orange flower water. In a large bowl, whisk egg whites until stiff, add remaining sugar and whisk again.

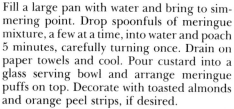

Fill a large pan with water and bring to simmering point. Drop spoonfuls of meringue mixture, a few at a time, into water and poach 5 minutes, carefully turning once. Drain on paper towels and cool. Pour custard into a glass serving bowl and arrange meringue puffs on top. Decorate with toasted almonds and orange peel strips, if desired.

Makes 4 servings.

Creamy Cranberry Fool

1/2 (12-oz.) package fresh cranberries
1/3 cup orange juice
3/4 cup superfine sugar
1-1/4 cups whipping cream
Grated orange peel, additional fresh
    cranberries and fresh leaves to decorate, if
    desired

In a saucepan, combine cranberries, orange juice and sugar. Simmer about 10 minutes, until berries pop; cool.

When cranberries are cold, using a wooden spoon, press through a fine metal sieve. In a large bowl, whip cream until stiff and fold in cranberry puree; chill.

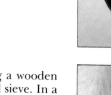

Spoon fool into individual dessert dishes and decorate with grated orange peel, additional fresh cranberries and fresh leaves, if desired.

Makes 4 servings.

VARIATION: Substitute 1/2 pound of plums for cranberries. Cook plums with 3 tablespoons of water and omit orange juice.

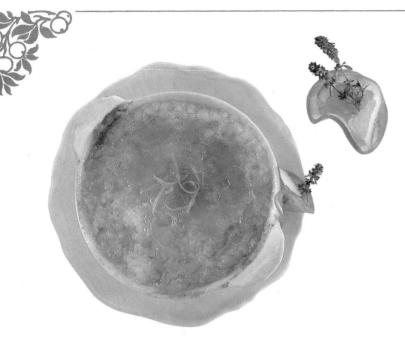

Caramel Rice

1/3 cup uncooked white short-grain rice
2-1/2 cups milk
1 vanilla bean
1/2 cup half and half
Juice of 1 orange
Superfine sugar
Shredded orange peel, orange slices and fresh
  herbs to garnish, if desired

In a saucepan, combine rice and milk and add vanilla bean. Simmer over very low heat 45 minutes to 1 hour, until rice is soft and creamy.

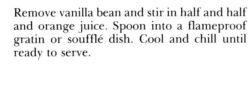

Remove vanilla bean and stir in half and half and orange juice. Spoon into a flameproof gratin or soufflé dish. Cool and chill until ready to serve.

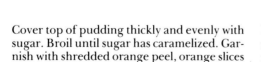

Cover top of pudding thickly and evenly with sugar. Broil until sugar has caramelized. Garnish with shredded orange peel, orange slices and fresh herbs, if desired, and serve at once.

Makes 4 servings.

NOTE: If desired, chill pudding again before serving, but serve within 2 hours.

Queen of Puddings

2 cups milk
2/3 cup half and half
Grated peel of 1 small lemon
1-1/2 cups fresh white bread crumbs
3 tablespoons butter
1-1/4 cups superfine sugar
3 small eggs, separated
3 tablespoons raspberry jam
Orange slices, fresh raspberries and fresh
  herbs to garnish, if desired

Preheat oven to 350F (175C). Butter and oval flameproof dish. In a saucepan, combine milk, half and half and lemon peel.

Heat milk mixture gently 5 minutes, then remove from heat and let stand 5 minutes to infuse. Place bread crumbs, butter and 1/4 of sugar in a bowl; pour warm milk on top. Stir until butter and sugar are dissolved. In a small bowl, beat egg yolks, then stir into bread crumb mixture. Pour into buttered dish and bake 45 to 50 minutes, until set. Remove from oven and cool slightly. Warm raspberry jam and spread over pudding.

Reduce oven temperature to 325F (165C). In a large bowl, whisk egg whites until stiff, then fold in remaining sugar. Pile meringue on pudding and return to oven about 20 minutes, until meringue is crisp and golden. Serve warm or cold. Garnish with orange slices, fresh raspberries and herbs, if desired.

Makes 4 servings.

NOTE: Sieve raspberry jam to remove seeds, if desired.

Bread & Fruit Pudding

3/4 cup raisins and currants, mixed
8 thin slices white bread, buttered
2 tablespoons candied fruit, chopped
Superfine sugar

Custard:
1 egg yolk
1-1/4 cups milk
2/3 cup half and half
1 vanilla bean
1 teaspoon superfine sugar

In a bowl, cover raisins and currants with water; let stand to swell. Preheat oven to 350F (175C). Grease an oval baking dish.

Cut crusts from bread and sandwich 4 slices together. Cut in 4 squares and place in greased dish. Drain fruit and sprinkle fruit and chopped candied fruit over bread. Top with remaining bread, buttered side up.

To prepare custard, place egg yolk in a large glass measure. In a saucepan, combine milk, half and half, vanilla bean and sugar and bring almost to boiling point. Pour over egg, stir, then strain into dish, pouring down sides so top slices of bread are not soaked. Let stand 30 minutes. Sprinkle with sugar and place in a roasting pan. Pour in enough boiling water to come halfway up sides of dish and bake 45 to 50 minutes, until top is golden-brown. Serve immediately.

Makes 4 servings.

Strawberry Shortcake

8 tablespoons butter, softened
1/4 cup superfine sugar
1-1/4 cups all-purpose flour
3 tablespoons cornstarch
2-1/4 cups strawberries, sliced
3 tablespoons red currant jelly
1-1/4 cups whipping cream
Additional sliced strawberries and mint leaves to garnish, if desired

In a bowl, cream butter and sugar until light and fluffy. Sift flour and cornstarch into creamy mixture and stir to make a firm dough.

Wrap in foil and chill 30 minutes. Preheat oven to 350F (175C). Place dough on a baking sheet and pat or roll to a circle about 1/2 inch thick. Prick all over with a fork and bake about 20 minutes, until lightly golden. Cool on baking sheet.

Carefully transfer shortcake to a serving plate and cover with whole strawberries. In a small saucepan, melt red currant jelly and brush over strawberries. In a bowl, whip cream until stiff. Using a pastry bag fitted with a star nozzle, pipe a border of whipped cream around edge of shortcake. Serve within 1 hour. Garnish with additional sliced strawberries and mint leaves, if desired. Makes 6 to 8 servings.

Atholl Brose

3 tablespoons regular rolled oats
1/3 cup whole blanched almonds
1-1/4 cups whipping cream
1/4 cup whiskey
1/4 cup orange flower honey
1 tablespoon lemon juice

Toast oats under broiler until brown. Toast almonds under broiler to brown evenly and chop finely.

In a large bowl, whip cream to soft peaks, then gradually whisk in whiskey, honey and lemon juice.

Fold oats and 1/2 of chopped almonds into creamy mixture and spoon into 4 dessert dishes. Chill. To serve, sprinkle remaining almonds on top of each pudding.

Makes 4 servings.

NOTE: This is a traditional Scottish dessert—delicious and very rich.

Cream & Sugar Parfaits

1-1/4 cups whipping cream
1 cup plain yogurt
1-1/2 cups packed light-brown sugar
Fresh strawberries or raspberries to serve, if desired

In a large bowl, whip cream to stiff peaks. Fold in yogurt.

Half fill 4 glasses with creamy mixture. Sprinkle with about 1/3 of brown sugar. Spoon remaining creamy mixture into glasses, then pile on remaining brown sugar.

Refrigerate overnight. Serve puddings with fresh strawberries or raspberries, if desired.

Makes 4 servings.

NOTE: The brown sugar melts and forms a fudgy layer in these parfaits. They must be prepared a day in advance to allow for this.

Dacquoise

1 cup whole blanched almonds
5 egg whites
1-1/2 cups superfine sugar
2-3/4 cups dried apricots
Juice of 1 lemon
Water
1-1/2 cups whipping cream
Toasted sliced almonds and fresh herbs to
    decorate, if desired

Toast whole almonds under a broiler, until evenly browned. Cool, then grind finely in a coffee grinder or a food processor fitted with the metal blade. Set aside. Preheat oven to 300F (150C). Line a baking sheet with parchment paper.

In a large bowl, whisk egg whites until stiff but not dry. Sprinkle with 2 tablespoons of sugar and whisk 1 minute. Using a metal spoon, fold in ground almonds and remaining sugar. Spoon meringue onto prepared baking sheet and spread evenly to a 10-inch circle. Bake 1-1/2 to 2 hours, until dry and light brown. Peel off paper and cool on a wire rack.

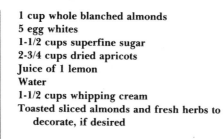

Place apricots and lemon juice in a saucepan. Cover with water and simmer over medium heat about 30 minutes, until tender; cool. In food processor, process apricots and a small amount of cooking liquid to make a thick puree. In a small bowl, whip cream stiffly and fold 1/2 of puree into whipped cream. Pile onto meringue and drizzle remaining puree over top. If necessary, thin puree with additional cooking liquid. Decorate with toasted almonds and fresh herbs, if desired.

Makes 6 to 8 servings.

Cherry Clafouti

1-1/2 pounds pitted dark sweet cherries, thawed
    and drained if frozen
3/4 cup all-purpose flour
Pinch of salt
3 eggs
1/3 cup superfine sugar
2 cups milk
1 tablespoon cherry brandy or kirsch
Powdered sugar

Preheat oven to 400F (205C). Butter an oval baking dish and place cherries in it.

Sift flour and salt into a small bowl. In a large bowl, beat eggs and sugar until creamy, then fold in flour and salt. In a saucepan, warm milk slightly over low heat and stir milk and cherry brandy or kirsch into egg mixture. Beat well until batter is smooth, then pour batter over cherries.

Bake 30 minutes, until set and golden. Serve warm dusted with powdered sugar.

Makes 6 servings.

NOTE: Fresh cherries can taste a little bland when cooked. Add 1 to 2 drops almond extract to improve the flavor, if desired.

Chocolate Pears

2 ounces amaretti cookies (macaroons)
3 to 4 tablespoons Cointreau
4 ounces semisweet chocolate
3 tablespoons strong coffee
1 tablespoon orange juice
2 tablespoons butter
2 eggs, separated
4 ripe medium-size pears
Orange peel curls and fresh mint to garnish, if
    desired

Place amaretti cookies in a bowl. Pour liqueur over cookies. Using end of a rolling pin, crush cookies to rough crumbs.

In top of a double boiler or a bowl set over a pan of simmering water, melt chocolate with coffee and orange juice, stirring until smooth. Remove from heat and beat in butter and egg yolks. In a separate bowl, whisk egg whites until stiff and fold chocolate mixture into them. Set aside. Peel pears, leaving them whole with stems in tact. Hollow out as much core as possible from bottom and fill cavity with crumb mixture.

Set pears on a wire rack, cutting off a small slice to make them stand upright, if necessary. Spoon chocolate mixture over pears to coat evenly. Chill several hours or overnight. To serve, place on individual plates. Garnish with orange peel and mint, if desired.

Makes 4 servings.

Minty Chocolate Mousse

6 ounces semisweet chocolate
1-1/4 cups whipping cream
1 egg
Pinch of salt
Few drops peppermint extract
Coarsely grated semisweet chocolate to decorate,
    if desired

Sugared Mint Leves:
Mint leaves
1 small egg white
Superfine sugar

Break up chocolate in small pieces and place in a blender or food processor fitted with the metal blade.

In a small saucepan, heat whipping cream until almost boiling. Pour cream over chocolate and blend 1 minute. Add egg, salt and peppermint extract and blend 1 minute more. Pour into individual ramekin dishes and refrigerate overnight.

To prepare decoration, wash and dry mint leaves. In a shallow bowl, lightly whisk egg white and dip in mint leaves to cover. Dip leaves into sugar, shake off any excess and let stand on waxed paper until hardened. To serve, decorate mousses with sugared mint leaves and grated chocolate, if desired. Makes 4 to 6 servings.

Note: Peppermint extract has a very strong flavor; use it sparingly.

Apple Charlotte

1-1/2 pounds tart eating apples
1/2 cup packed light-brown sugar
8 tablespoons butter
Grated peel of 1 lemon
2-1/2 cups coarse fresh bread crumbs
Apple slices and fresh mint to decorate, if
  desired

Peel, core and slice apples. In a saucepan, place sliced apples, 1/3 cup of brown sugar, 2 tablespoons of butter and grated lemon peel. Simmer, covered, over low heat until soft. Beat until pureed.

In a skillet, melt remaining butter and sauté bread crumbs until golden-brown, stirring constantly to prevent burning. Stir in remaining brown sugar and cool.

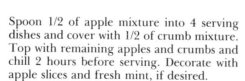

Spoon 1/2 of apple mixture into 4 serving dishes and cover with 1/2 of crumb mixture. Top with remaining apples and crumbs and chill 2 hours before serving. Decorate with apple slices and fresh mint, if desired.

Makes 4 servings.

NOTE: To prevent brown sugar from hardening when stored, place a slice of apple in the container with it, and the brown sugar will stay soft.

Summer Puddings

8 ounces red currants
8 ounces black currants
Juice of 1/2 orange
1/2 cup superfine sugar
1-2/3 cups fresh raspberries
12 to 16 thin slices white bread
Additional red currants to garnish, if desired

In a saucepan, combine currants, orange juice and sugar. Cook over low heat, stirring occasionally, until currants are juicy and just tender. Gently stir in 1-2/3 cups raspberries; cool.

Cut crusts from bread. From 6 slices, line 6 ramekin dishes or dariole molds, overlapping bread to line dishes completely. From remaining bread, cut circles same size as top of small ramekin dishes or dariole molds. Strain fruit, reserving juice, and spoon fruit into bread-lined dishes, pressing down quite firmly. Cover with bread circles. Pour some of reserved juice into dishes to soak bread. Place a small weight on top of each pudding.

Chill puddings and remaining juice several hours or overnight. To serve, turn puddings out onto individual plates and spoon a small amount of reserved juices over them. Garnish with additional red currants, if desired.

Makes 6 servings.

NOTE: A dariole mold is a small cylindrical mold used for cooking pastries or vegetables.

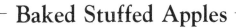

Flaming Fruit Salad

1 pound mixed dried fruit such as prunes,
   apricots, figs, apples, pears and peaches
   (7-1/2 cups)
2-1/2 cups water
2 tablespoons sherry
Juice of 1/2 lemon
2 tablespoons honey
1/2 (3-inch) cinnamon stick
1/4 cup brandy
3/4 cup toasted sliced almonds
1/2 cup walnuts, coarsely chopped
Fresh herbs to garnish, if desired

Soak dried fruit overnight in water and sherry.

In a saucepan, place fruit and soaking liquid, lemon juice, honey and cinnamon stick. Cover and simmer over low heat until fruit is just tender. Discard cinnamon stick, transfer fruit to a serving dish and keep warm.

In a small pan, heat brandy and light. While still flaming, pour over fruit and sprinkle with almonds and walnuts. Garnish with fresh herbs, if desired, and serve immediately.

Makes 5 to 6 servings.

NOTE: The effect of flaming brandy is to burn off the alcohol and so concentrate the flavor. It is important to warm brandy first or it will not light.

Baked Stuffed Apples

3 tablespoons dark raisins
3 tablespoons golden raisins
1/4 cup plus 1 tablespoon ginger wine, Madeira
   or sweet sherry
4 large baking apples
3/4 cup toasted sliced almonds
1 to 2 tablespoons orange marmalade
Chilled whipped cream to serve

Preheat oven to 350F (175C). In a small bowl, combine raisins and ginger wine, Madeira or sweet sherry. Let stand several hours.

Wash and dry apples; do not peel. Core apples and score a line around middle of each apple. Place in an ovenproof dish. Drain raisins, reserving liquid. In a bowl, mix raisins, almonds and marmalade and fill apple cavities with fruit and nut mixture, pushing mixture down firmly. Pour strained liquid over apples.

Bake apples 45 minutes to 1 hour, until soft. Spoon a dollop of whipped cream on top of each apple and serve immediately.

Makes 4 servings.

Cream Cheese Strudel

3/4 cup chopped hazelnuts
1 (8-oz.) pkg. cream cheese, softened
2 tablespoons superfine sugar
1 egg
Grated peel of 1 lemon
5 sheets filo pastry, thawed if frozen
4 tablespoons butter, melted
black currants and mint leaves to garnish, if desired

Preheat oven to 400F (205C). Generously grease a baking sheet. Toast hazelnuts to brown evenly; cool.

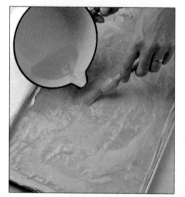

In a bowl, beat cream cheese, sugar, egg and lemon peel until smooth. Beat in toasted hazelnuts. Place 1 sheet of pastry on greased baking sheet, keeping remainder covered with a damp tea towel. Brush with melted butter and place another sheet on top. Layer all 5 sheets of pastry, brushing each one with melted butter.

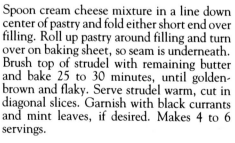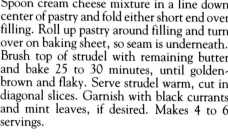

Spoon cream cheese mixture in a line down center of pastry and fold either short end over filling. Roll up pastry around filling and turn over on baking sheet, so seam is underneath. Brush top of strudel with remaining butter and bake 25 to 30 minutes, until golden-brown and flaky. Serve strudel warm, cut in diagonal slices. Garnish with black currants and mint leaves, if desired. Makes 4 to 6 servings.

Nectarine Baklava

10 sheets filo pastry, thawed if frozen
2/3 cup butter, melted
1-3/4 cups chopped mixed nuts
1-1/2 teaspoons ground cinnamon
1/2 cup superfine sugar
Grated peel and juice of 2 lemons
1 tablespoon orange flower water
4 nectarines
Powdered sugar
Nectarine slices and fresh herbs to garnish, if desired

Preheat oven to 350F (175C). Cut pastry sheets in half, then cut each half in quarters.

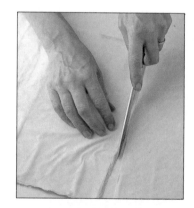

Working quickly, brush 1 cut sheet of pastry with melted butter. Line 8 individual 4-inch pans with 1 piece of pastry. Brush 3 more cut sheets with butter and lay cut pieces into pans, overlapping each other at different angles. In a bowl, combine nuts, cinnamon and 1/2 of sugar; spread 1/2 of nut mixture over pastry. Cover with 2 more layers of pastry, each brushed with butter, then top with remaining nut mixture. Cover with remaining pastry, brushed with butter.

Press down pastry in pans and bake 20 to 25 minutes, until golden-brown. Meanwhile, in a saucepan, combine remaining sugar and lemon juice. Cook, over low heat, until sugar dissolves. Stir in lemon peel and orange flower water. Bring to a boil and simmer 3 minutes; cool slightly. Slice nectarines into syrup, turning carefully to coat. Spoon into center of pastries and dust edges with powdered sugar. Serve lukewarm or cold, when pastries have absorbed some syrup. Garnish with nectarine slices and fresh herbs, if desired.

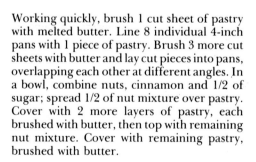

Makes 8 servings.

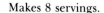

Tarte Francaise

13 ounces fresh or frozen puff pastry
1 egg yolk, beaten
1/4 cup plus 2 tablespoons apricot jam, sieved
2 tablespoons lemon juice
1-1/2 pounds mixed fresh fruit such as grapes,
   strawberries, raspberries and bananas
Additional strawberries and leaves to garnish,
   if desired

Thaw pastry, if frozen, and roll out to a 12" x 8" rectangle. Fold pastry in half. Cut a rectangle from folded edge 1-1/2 inches in from outside edges.

Unfold middle section and roll out to a 12" x 8" rectangle. Place on a baking sheet, dampen edges with water, then unfold frame and place carefully on top of pastry rectangle. Press edges of pastry together. Mark a pattern on frame and brush with beaten egg yolk. Prick center all over.

Preheat oven to 425F (220C). Chill pastry 10 minutes, then bake about 20 minutes, until golden-brown; cool. In a saucepan, heat jam and lemon juice gently until jam has melted. Halve and seed grapes. Leave strawberries and raspberries whole and peel and slice bananas. Brush bottom of tart lightly with jam and arrange prepared fruit in rows. Brush fruit with jam and garnish with additional strawberries and leaves, if desired. Serve as soon as possible.

Makes 6 servings.

Austrian Cheesecake

4 tablespoons butter, softened
2/3 cup superfine sugar
1 cup plus 1 tablespoon cottage cheese, sieved
2 eggs, separated
1/2 cup ground almonds
1/3 cup fine semolina
Grated peel and juice of 1 small lemon
Powered sugar
Lemon twists to garnish, if desired

Preheat oven to 375F (190C). Butter a deep 8-inch cake pan and dust with flour. In a large bowl, cream butter, sugar and cottage cheese until soft and fluffy.

Beat egg yolks into cheese mixture, then fold in ground almonds, semolina and lemon peel and juice. In a separate bowl, whisk egg whites until stiff and carefully fold into cottage cheese mixture.

Turn mixture into buttered pan and bake about 50 minutes, until golden-brown and springy to touch. Cool 20 minutes in pan, then turn out and dust with powdered sugar. Serve cheesecake warm. Garnish with lemon twists, if desired. Makes 6 servings.

Note: If desired, place a paper doily on cheesecake, then dust with powdered sugar. Remove doily and serve.

INDEX

Aioli & Crudités 21
Almond-Cheese Balls 18
Amaretti Mousse 86
Apple Charlotte 92
Artichoke & Cheese Pizza 47
Asparagus with Avocado Dressing 56
Asparagus Crepes 34
Asparagus Rolls 23
Atholl Brose 89
Austrian Cheesecake 95
Avocado & Camembert Omelet 81

Baked Potato Layer 73
Baked Stuffed Apples 93
Basic Crepes 32
Basic Omelet 36
Beer Fondue 62
Beet & Onion Salad 51
Blue Cheese Dip & Crackers 70
Bran Crackers 70
Bread & Fruit Pudding 88
Brie & Fig Tempter 76
Broccoli & Cauliflower Crumble 71
Broccoli Pasta Soufflé 42
Brussel Sprouts with Almonds 71
Buck Rarebit 82
Buckwheat Noodles with Eggs 74

Caramel Rice 87
Caribbean Creole Sauce 28
Carrot & Cilantro Soup 13
Cauliflower Fritters 64
Celery & Stilton Soup 8
Cheddar Cheese Crackers 70
Cheese & Onion Pastries 17
Cheese Filo Pastries 19
Cheesy Bread 80
Cherry Clafouti 90
Chocolate Pears 91
Chow Mein Salad 57
Classic Swiss Fondue 59
Clear Vegetable Soup 14
Coconut Lime Dressing 53
Cream & Sugar Parfaits 89
Cream Cheese Bites 78
Cream Cheese Strudel 94
Cream of Broccoli Soup 16
Cream of Carrot Soup 12
Creamed Spinach & Celery 72
Creamy Celery & Onion Soup 15
Creamy Cranberry Fool 86

Crème Brûlée 84
Crepes with Corn-Cheese Sauce 34
Crispy Coated Vegetables 75
Curried Cheese Fondue 59
Curried Omelet 36
Curried Vegetable Envelopes 26

Dacquoise 90
Deep-Fried Camembert 20
Dhal 30
Dolmades 24
Dutch Fondue 60

Egg & Mushroom Benedict 80
Eggplant & Tomato Pizza 46
Eggplant Tahini Pâté 67

Fennel & Walnut Soup 7
Feta Cheese Kebabs 25
Flaming Fruit Salad 93
Florentine Omelet 37
Fluffy Cheese Omelet 38
Four Cheese Pizza 46
French Toast Fingers 78
French Turnip Soup 13
Friar's Omelet 39
Fruit Casket 104

Gazpacho Dressing 54
Glazed Carrots & Onions 73
Golden Vegetable Soup 15
Gooseberry Icecream 85
Grapefruit Cheesecake 88
Greek Dressing 55
Greek Salad Pitas 77
Guacamole 68

Harvest Barley Soup 10
Herb Cucumber Frais 56
Herb Popovers with Buttered Eggs 81
Highland Fondue 63

Indian Country Frittata 40
Italian Omelet 37

Jade Salad 49

Leek & Onion Calzone 47

Malaysian Salad 48
Marinara Sauce 28

Marinated Artichokes 22
Marinated Mushrooms 23
Marinated Mushrooms with
    Grapefruit 26
Marinated Stuffed Leaves 43
Mediterranean Sauce 41
Mexican Bean Dip 22
Mexican Bean Soup 9
Minorcan Vegetable Soup 11
Minty Chocolate Mousse 91
Mixed Leaf Salad 58
Mixed Vegetable Kabobs 64
Mozzarella Crouton Crepes 33
Mushroom Bundles 83
Mushroom Crepes 35
Mushroom Curry 30
Mushroom Dip 55
Mushroom Pasties 24
Mushroom Roll 83
Mushrooms & Blue Cheese 17

Nectarine Baklava 94
Normandy Fondue 62
Nutty-Crumb Cream 85

Oeufs à La Neige 86
Onion & Mushroom Bhajis 67
Orange & Sesame Seed Dressing 53

Parmesan Crepes 33
Peanut-Banana Sandwich 79
Peanut Sauce 21
Pears Stuffed with Gorgonzola 69
Peppers with Cauliflower 29
Peppery Mozzarella Salad 25
Pesto Sauce 27
Pistou 16
Potage Bonne Femme 10
Potato & Herb Omelet 38
Potato Salad 58
Potato Skins with Sour Cream 69
Potato Waffles with Mushrooms 82
Potted Herb Cheese 19
Pub Fondue 61
Puffy Cottage Cheese Omelet 39

Queen of Puddings 87

Ratatouille 44
Roquefort Grape Relish Sandwich 76
Rosé Fondue 61

Saffron & Pistachio Dressing 54
Savory Soufflé Omelet 40
Sesame Cheese Balls 18
Somerset Fondue 60
Soufflé Potatoes 72
Spanakopita 68
Spiced Okra 44
Spicy Chickpea Balls 65
Spicy Lentil Soup 9
Spicy Sesame Noodles 74
Spinach & Feta Rolls 20
Spinach Crepes 35
Sprouted Bean Salad 49
Stilton & Walnut Salad 48
Strawberry Shortcake 88
Summer Puddings 92
Summer Vegetable Salad 57
Swiss Potatoes 65

Tabbouleh 50
Tamil Nadu Vegetables 29
Tarragon & Tomato Soup 12
Tarte Francaise 95
Three Pepper Pizza 45
Tomato & Rice Soup 8
Tomato Sauce 27
Traditional Pizza Dough 45
Tropical Flummery 84
Tropical Shortcake 79

Vegetable Coucous 31
Vegetable Kebabs 43
Vegetable Samosa 66
Vegetarian Bolognese Sauce 42
Vegetarian Lentil Medley 31

Waldorf Salad 50
Watercress & Almond Soup 7
Welsh Fondue 63
Welsh Rarebit 77
Whole Wheat Crepes 32
Whole Wheat Pasta Salad 51
Winter Green Salad 51
Winter Red Salad 52
Winter Vegetable Soup 14

Zucchini & Pasta Mold 41
Zucchini & Tomato Soup 11